TALES FROM THE BULLY BOX

TALES FROM THE BULLY BOX

EDITED BY CAT WOODS

Tales from the Bully Box

Copyright © 2014 Elephant's Bookshelf Press, LLC

Editor: Cat Woods
Cover Design: Sarah Tregay
Book Design: R.C. Lewis

Elephant's Bookshelf Press, LLC
Springfield, NJ 07081
www.elephantsbookshelfpress.com

ISBN-13: 978-1-940180-06-9

Table of Contents

Once Bullied, Now BRAVE

For over a year, I woke up every morning and dreaded going to school, because I knew the bully would be there. I went through each day, trying to stay under her radar so I wouldn't get noticed and picked on. I would come home crying from the events that happened during the day. But then I realized I was doing it all wrong. I decided I wanted to be BRAVE. From that day on, I woke up confident, and I looked forward to going to school, because I knew things were going to change.

I took a stand against the bully instead of trying to go unnoticed. I encouraged others to stand with me, and our actions started a spark that grew into a flame—a flame that currently burns brighter and stronger than any bully's blaze. We are gathering an army to stand up for those who need help. Our troops extend throughout communities.

Teachers, principals, police officers, parents, and friends are our allies. We are part of something bigger than ourselves. We are a unit that cares for each other, fights for each, and supports each other.

You do not have to go through this alone. Reach out to your community, take a stand for yourself and others who need it, Build Relationships Against Violence Everywhere.

I am BRAVE. Are you?

Alexandra Wacker
Founder of the BRAVE anti-bullying program

Real Help for Real Problems

For the first time in over thirty years of teaching I have seen a program that empowered my students to take a stand against bullying. Bullying is something that has been around since before I became a teacher, but the BRAVE program is new. BRAVE stands for Building Relationships Against Violence Everywhere and was started in response to the hurtful atmosphere found in our schools. Every month, two high school students worked with my class to build a "unit" that would stand together give students ideas to use when they were bullied or saw bullying taking place.

I still remember the morning one of my students came in very upset after getting off the bus. There was a young boy getting bullied to the point of tears and my student wanted to do something about it. So we talked about the BRAVE ideas. The next morning four of my students met me in the hallway with excitement, because what they tried worked! They felt so empowered and encouraged to continue fighting bullying everywhere. Obviously, I have heard numerous stories from my students about what they are doing to stop bullying since then. Our school and our community is a better place, but we all need to continue to be BRAVE.

Nancy Siebenahler
Elementary Teacher

Making the World
a Better Place,
One Story
at a Time

As a child advocate, a mom, a speech coach, a math tutor, and a former preschool teacher and youth director, I know kids. I write for kids, I work with kids, and I raise kids. I know the pitfalls that each age brings, and I know the effort it takes to reach your potential, no matter what that might be. I know how hard it is to put yourself into the world to be accepted or rejected on somebody else's whim. Because of this, I also know what bullying looks like, sounds like, and feels like.

I know how damaging it can be. I know that kids who are bullied struggle in school. I know that kids who are teased think they can't do anything right. I know that picking on someone can change who they are and what they would have become.

More importantly, I know that bullying can be stopped.

We all have decisions to make. Every day, we choose to be nice or mean. We choose to offer a helping hand or to walk on by. We choose to start rumors or to stop them. Each day, one thousand times a day, we choose how we will act toward those around us. These moments are our stories, and the endings are a direct result of the choices we make.

There is no magic bullet or school program or no-tolerance policy in the world that can stop bullying until we choose to stop it. Change starts with us. Kindness starts with us. Building relationships against violence everywhere, every day, starts with each one of us individually.

Four years ago, my daughter was bullied so badly she begged to be home-schooled rather than face the students who tormented her. Three years ago, she stood up for herself against the ringleader who made her life miserable. Two years ago, she created a program for a fourth grade class to teach kids how to work together and look out for each other. One year ago, that program was expanded to all classes in grades 3-5. This year, an anthology of short stories will be published to honor the lessons she, the students, the teachers and the community learned because of her experiences.

Within BRAVE, kids learned to trust teachers when they had problems. They learned the difference between getting their feelings hurt and being bullied. They learned how to intervene when someone was being picked on. They learned how to talk to their parents and how to say, "No." They learned respect—for themselves, for each other and for their teachers. They became a community—a unit—that worked together.

Creating a community built on trust and respect is

the only way to stop bullying in its tracks. But that starts with a single choice and the resulting story.

As a writer, I wanted to show how we are all responsible for the way we behave. I wanted to show how being a bystander can be just as hurtful to someone as being a bully is. I wanted readers—kids, parents, teachers, and principals alike—to see the impact that simple choices can make on those around them.

As the editor for *Tales from the Bully Box*, I wanted to share the work of amazing authors who work hard to make this world a stronger, safer place for everyone regardless of where they come from or what they look like. In the process, I chose ordinary stories with ordinary characters, because bullying is an ordinary event that happens to ordinary people. But this BRAVE-inspired anthology isn't about bullying. It's about making little choices and doing kind things that turn ordinary moments into something extraordinary.

As the ten tales from this bully box demonstrate, there is no single solution to bullying. Rather, it is the culmination of the things we say, the things we do and the way we treat others.

Day by day, person by person, bullying stops when we change the world one story at a time.

Cat Woods
Author, Editor, Supporter of all things good

Publisher's
Note

With *Tales From the Bully Box*, Elephant's Bookshelf Press embarks on a new adventure, and I'm thrilled that you've joined us. As you can see on the cover, this book is part of our "Colors for a Cause" collection. The anthologies in the collection will each have a unifying theme, a cause if you will. In this case, the theme is anti-bullying. We hope teachers will find value in this anthology and that it will help lay the foundation for healthy classroom discussions. To encourage such discussion, I will provide discounts for teachers' orders. Please contact us via publisher@elephants-bookshelfpress.com

Although it is a for-profit publisher, EBP has the soul of a nonprofit organization. We endeavor to help talented writers achieve their goals of publication and developing an audience. At the same time, we have found ourselves working with authors who want more than simple publication: our authors aim to make a difference. For example, the proceeds from our novel *Battery Brothers* by Steven Carman (who also has a story in this collection) will go to the Sunshine Foundation, which was the first wish-granting organization in the United States.

In addition, a portion of the proceeds from *Tales from the Bully Box*—both electronic and print versions—will be donated to organizations working to rid our schools of bullying. It's not an easy job. And I won't pretend I know the best way to do it. Determining which organizations are doing it well will likely remain an ongoing assessment. That's ok: We're in it for the long haul and elephants never forget.

Again, thank you for joining us on this journey. To find out what else you can do to make a difference in this cause, you can visit The Bully Box website at www.thebullybox.com. If you have questions or suggestions along the way, please let us know.

Matt Sinclair
President, Chief Elephant Officer

Hailey's Shooting Star

STEVEN CARMAN

I DRIBBLED MY PINK BASKETBALL on a quiet side street in the burbs. Strong summer rays seared the back of my neck. My sweaty T-shirt clung to me like second skin. I cut to the spray-painted foul line and eyed the hoop, a portable one with a round steel pole, glass backboard, and a heavy-duty base that edged the curb. I cupped the basketball in my right hand and heaved a hook shot.

Swish.

Nothing but net.

Too bad nobody was around to see me sink it. Still, I imagined a crowd chanting, *Go, Hailey! Go, Hailey!*

I was practicing by myself two houses down from my aunt and uncle's new home. Per my aunt, the hoop was her neighbor's and everyone was welcome to use it. That was music to my ears.

Shooting a basketball was a lot easier when I had a left hand to help guide my shots. But my accuracy was improving. Day by day. Practice by practice.

Three years ago, when I was nine, I had luckily injured my left hand while playing in a basketball game. Yeah, I said *luckily injured* because it gave doctors the opportunity to examine it. They discovered something on the X-ray—eventually diagnosed as osteosarcoma, a fancy name for a type of bone cancer. It was the hand they eventually amputated. Done to remove the cancer. Done to trash it like moldy bread.

So now I had only one hand. My left arm was shorter than my right, stubbed at my forearm. Which was okay. I was healthy now—cancer free. All the body parts I needed to keep playing the game I loved were intact.

Two boys approached from down the block. They looked to be about my age. I had no clue who they were.

The taller boy wore a muscle shirt over his wiry frame. His sidekick had a stocky build and was unsuccessfully spinning a basketball on his finger.

"What's up, guys?" I asked.

"S'up," the taller one said, blatantly staring at my stubbed arm.

Embarrassed, I glanced at the pavement. "I'm Hailey."

The shorter one dribbled the basketball between his legs. "I'm Matt. This is Jason. Did you just move here or something?"

"No. My aunt and uncle did. My mom and I are just helping them get set up. We'll be heading back upstate in a week."

"Cool," Jason said. "You mind getting off our court now? I wanna play Matt one-on-one."

I half smiled. "Seriously?"

Jason stole the basketball away from Matt mid-dribble and laid the ball up into the hoop. "Seriously. The Special Olympics are one block down."

Matt laughed, his body arching forward.

I dribbled my ball, the bounces hard and high. "Not nice."

Jason dished their ball back to Matt. "Sorry, girlie. I'd say you could play. But no girls are allowed on this court. Especially girls with only one hand. You might hurt yourself, y'know?"

I kept my chin up, my stare hard, even though my insides felt ripped.

A scrawny boy, twelvish, wandered out of a driveway two houses down. He had a mess of curly black hair. His thumbs worked a large black remote controller. Through thick eyeglasses, he peered at a toy truck making 360s in the street.

"I'll take that kid on my team," I said. "We'll play you guys. If we win, you leave and let us shoot around. If you win, I'll go back inside and let you guys play your game. Deal?"

Jason laughed obnoxiously, his hands covering his mouth. "You wanna play with Peanut? That loser couldn't hit the backboard if he tried."

"Yes, I want Peanut."

Jason walked up to me, wagging his finger. "Sorry, I forgot about another rule. Losers can't play on this court either."

I raised an eyebrow. "You're scared to play us."

Jason made a face. "Yeah right. Get lost."

I rolled my eyes. "Seems like you're scared to me."

Jason's jaw dropped. "Fine. We'll play you guys up to seven. We'll use our ball, not that girlie pink one you got. We'll be done with you quick and easy." He cupped his hands around his mouth. "Yo, Peanut. Let's go. We need you to play. You're on her team."

Shoulders slumped, Peanut walked toward us. He parked his toy truck and set his controller down on the curb. "But you said I was never allowed to play on this court."

Jason folded his lanky arms. "I'll make this one exception, Peanut."

I dribbled my ball over to Peanut. "Do you want to play?"

"Sure, I love basketball, but they never let me," he said, looking at the ground. The toe of his new sneaker kicked at a pebble. "I'm just not very good."

"Forget them," I said. "Play if you want to. I'm Hailey. I'll assume your real name isn't Peanut."

A light blush crept into his cheeks. "I hate that nickname. I'm Pete."

"Hi, Pete. Nice to meet you."

"Nice to meet you, too. Let's play ball."

My plan was simple. Get Pete the ball. Let him shoot. Let him have some fun.

And that was what I did. I got him some clear looks at the basket, but his shots were erratic. He did manage to hit the rim. Once. A brick that almost took the rim down. But that didn't matter. He was doing what he loved. It bothered me, though, that Matt and Jason were laughing at his misses. Pete went silent, and I could tell he was getting down on himself.

In no time, we were losing 6-0.

"Is that a tear I see in your eye, Peanut?" Matt mocked. "Do you need a tissue?"

Pete blinked his eyes, wiggled his eyeglasses. "No, I don't need a tissue."

"Grow up," I said to Matt. "Pete's not crying. Even if he was, there's no shame in that. Even my dad, who's super tough, cries."

Matt and Jason slapped at each other's arms, laughing.

My blood boiled. My dad was my hero and if they only knew him, they wouldn't be so quick to laugh at him. I clapped Pete's shoulder. "Ignore them, buddy. Just have fun. If we lose, we lose. No big deal."

Pete smiled around braced teeth. "Cool. I wish there was a way to beat those guys, though. I'd love to win. Just once."

I whispered in his ear, "Do you mind if I get us back in this game? I have a pretty wicked hook shot."

Pete's eyes opened wide, like a bug. "Do it."

I knocked knuckles with him, then returned to guard Jason.

Jason checked the ball to me. "Game point," he said.

I checked it back.

I turned up the defense, smothering Jason. I stole the ball, spun around and charged in at the hoop. At the side of the key, I took a hook shot.

Swish.

I was feeling it. I was in the zone.

Jason and Matt were stunned.

I sank five more shots. All swishes.

They were no longer stunned. They were furious.

"Game point for us," I said, checking the ball to Jason.

"Double-team her," Jason said to Matt. "Don't let her shoot."

Matt and Jason got up on me.

I spied Pete alone near the basket, ready and waiting. I bounced a pass to him.

He bobbled the ball, focused on the rim, and heaved a shot. The ball clanked off the backboard and dropped right through the hoop.

Game over!

I ran over and slapped Pete five. "Great shot. You did it. You see, don't let anything or anybody stop you from doing what you love. Way to go. You're a star."

Pete flashed a thousand-watt smile. His cheeks pushed up to his eyes.

"Nice shot, Pete," Matt said. Small voice.

"Yeah, not too shabby, Pete," Jason added.

"Enough chitchat," I said, cueing my tough-girl voice. "Time for you guys to take your ball and get lost."

Matt's face went red and his arms flailed, like he was doing jumping jacks. "No way. We want a rematch."

"Stop," Jason said, his shoulders slumped. "A bet is a bet. Let's go."

I passed the ball to Jason. "I'm just kidding. Stay and play. But try and let Pete play more often. It's not fun being told you can't play, right?"

"Yeah, I see your point," Jason said. "I wish you were moving to here. We could use a great shooter like you on our team."

I gave Jason a tightlipped smile, flattered that he thought I had game.

Pete walked over to the curb and grabbed his remote and a piece of paper beside it. "Is this yours, Hailey?"

I patted the pocket on my shorts. *My photo.* My heart knocked like a shoe in a dryer. I didn't like people seeing me looking like I did in that photo. "Yeah, I'll take that," I said walking toward him.

"Is this you?" he asked, scrunching his nose.

I looked over Pete's shoulder at the photo. "Yeah, it's of my dad and me. He's overseas right now serving in the military. I haven't seen him in months."

I closed my eyes and recalled the day the photo was snapped. It was Easter in our backyard. I was nine, completely bald, in the midst of chemo. Chemo is a type of medical therapy that helped me fight the cancer, but it also caused me to temporarily lose my hair. My dad was also bald then, his hair removed by a razor and shaving cream. He told me that as long I couldn't have hair, he wouldn't either.

In the photo, a yellow shoulder-strapped dress hung loose on my tall, thin body. Dark circles underscored my hazelnut eyes. Skin, pale as porcelain, pulled tight across my high cheekbones. My dad, handsome and muscular, was gently holding my hand. The hand that doctors removed a few weeks later.

My dad managed a smile for the photo, but I saw the pain in his eyes. Nobody I knew was tougher than my dad. But when it came to me, his little girl, he was a mush. A big softie.

Matt and Jason gathered around and looked at the photo, too. Jason shuffled beside me. "If you don't mind me asking, how'd you lose your hand?"

In response to their muttered sorries, I told them that there was nothing to be sorry about. That I was cancer free and planned to live a long life.

My uncle's white cargo van passed us on the road. He parked in his driveway.

My heart beat fast. "Hey, you guys wanna see my aunt and uncle's new dog? My uncle just got it from a breeder."

We ran to the driveway. My uncle climbed out of the van. My mom and my aunt hurried out of the house, cameras in hand.

"Oh, I can't wait to see the pup," my mom said, breathing heavy.

"He's in the back. A real good boy, this one is," my uncle said and walked us to the rear of the van. When we gathered around, he pulled open the van doors.

There was no barking.

There was no dog.

There was just a ladder and some paint cans.

And my dad.

He was in his Army uniform.

Holding a bouquet of flowers.

My dad leaped out of the van and flashed me a smile so bright I could feel its glow.

I leaped into his arms with a scream. Tears streamed down my face.

My dad swung me around and I caught Jason's eye. He mouthed the word "later." Then, he grabbed Matt and Pete and the three of them headed toward the basketball court.

I felt complete. In every way.

My day was a perfect swish.

Questions

1. Jason and Matt had rules about who could play on the basketball court. Why were their rules unfair and a form of bullying?

2. What lessons do you think Jason and Matt learned from their encounter with Hailey?

3. What did Hailey do to boost Pete's confidence and self-esteem?

4. What was your favorite part of the story?

Every Camp
Has a Bully

CAT WOODS

THE IRON AND STONE GATE to Camp Crusoe shimmered in the headlights. It was the first manmade thing I'd seen in over an hour. Surrounded by pine trees taller than the skyscrapers back home, Camp Crusoe would be my prison for the summer. My parents had a choice—reading camp or summer school. They picked reading camp.

Not my choice at all.

On top of that, I was late. When I walked into Cabin 13, the other kids already had their bunks made up. The top two were taken. Only a bottom one remained. No way was I sleeping on a bottom bunk. I'd be the joke of the camp for sure.

I peered over the top bunk into the eyes of a kid half my size. Of course, everyone was smaller than my freakishly large frame, but I used that to my advantage. I had to. "Move it, Pipsqueak."

The kid opened and shut his mouth like a goldfish out of water. I'd seen the look before. Either he was terrified or he was making fun of me. He balled up his fists and said, "I was here first."

Obviously not afraid. A kid like that would make fun of me all summer long. Unless I put a stop to it first. "I don't care when you were here. This is my bunk. Get off and go somewhere else."

He didn't move. He just stared at me with those gray eyes.

"One. Two. Three," I counted, giving him another chance.

He snarked off instead. "What are you, my mom?"

I grabbed the edge of his mattress and shook it. "I'm your worst nightmare. Now move it, before I move you."

He jutted his chin out. "No."

He gave me no choice. I grabbed his arm and pulled him across the mattress. Not hard, mind you, but he yelped anyway.

Our cabin counselor, Rob, banged on the wall. "Everything all right in there?"

Rob's mattress springs squeaked. Footsteps followed. Everything happened in slow motion. My heart boxed at my ribs, bruising them. I couldn't get in trouble yet. Not on the first day. But the kid just glared at me, refusing to move. Rob knocked on the door. Tap. Tap. Tap.

I gritted my teeth and squeezed the kid's arm trying to get him to move. Because I would not—could not—sleep on a bottom bunk.

"Fine," the boy finally said. The door swung open.

Rob stepped in. "Hey, guys. Meet your new roomy, Ezekial."

Yeah, that was me. Ezekial. My parents named me after some prophet dude from the Bible who had visions and stuff. His name—our name—even meant something about God making us strong. I was strong all right. I could bench press other kids my age, and I had visions. Lots of them. Of needles poking into my arms. Of hospital beds and recovery rooms. Of getting teased constantly because I was a human Godzilla.

Sure, I was strong physically, but I think God did that because he knew I had a weak heart.

I unpacked my clothes and carefully hid my stuffed rabbit in my pillowcase where nobody would find it. When it was time for bed, I reached my hand between the flannel case and the pillow to stroke the satin of BunBun's ears. It was the only way I could sleep, and the reason I needed the top bunk.

A bugle call warbled in my ear. I rolled over and toppled out of bed onto the Pipsqueak below. Kyle's eyes shot daggers into me as he pushed me aside. He hated me. I could see the disgust on his face. My bunkmates bolted from the cabin, leaving me alone.

Welcome to reading camp, my friend.

Can I just say things never got better? Two weeks in, I wet the bed in the middle of the night. And the law of physics dictates that whatever is up must come down. Well, it leaked down on Kyle like a lukewarm shower.

Dear Mom,

Reading camp is way worse than summer school ever could have been. My cabinmates hate me—especially this kid named Kyle. Maybe you forgot how my medication makes me wet the bed. Kyle never will. I told you this would happen, but you didn't listen. And now, he won't leave me alone.

Your miserable son, Zeke.

The only good thing about camp was Sienna. She had red hair and a red personality. As in, she was a fireball. She made things fun. And even though she liked Kyle, she didn't hate me. She was sick, too. Sicker than me. As in, she might even die sick. Instead of working on our reading skills like the rest of the kids, Sienna and I worked on homework, trying to catch up to grade level, preparing for when the next medical emergency would keep us from school.

But Sienna's niceness only made Kyle hate me more. He did everything in his power to make me miserable. He dumped orange pop on my mattress so ants would attack, dropped eggshells in my pancakes when we were on cooking duty and booby-trapped the room whenever he had the chance. Finally, I left a dead mouse under his pillow to send a message. Dude, I'm done getting picked on.

His response? A maggoty fish in a pile of my laundry. No matter how many times I've washed my clothes, I still stink like moldy fish.

Which is why I used Kyle's bed instead of my own during free time. When he's off swimming with his friends and playing kissy face with Sienna, I read. Alone, in the quiet of the cabin with nobody to prank me. One day, I was so absorbed in the book I found on his bed that I didn't hear anyone come in. That was until Pipsqueak started yelling at me. In front of everyone.

"I'm sick of you, Zeke. Something is wrong with you. You need serious help."

"You don't know anything about me." I threw his book at him to get him to back off. He didn't have a clue. Worse, he didn't even care. His mission at reading camp was to torment me. When BunBun went missing, I knew Kyle was behind it.

The morning after my rabbit disappeared, I cornered him. "Where is it?"

"Where's what?" His lips sneered upward.

My stomach clenched like an iron fist was squeezing it. "You know."

"I don't know, and I don't care."

Told you I was right. I didn't need a prophet to know that every camp has a bully. The nights passed with me tossing and turning. I couldn't sleep without my stuffed rabbit. During the day, I hounded Kyle, trying to wear him down.

"What did you do with my stuff, Pipsqueak?"

He shook me off like he was trying to get rid of a mosquito. "For the one thousandth time, I have no idea what you're talking about."

I couldn't take it anymore. I leaned in close and choked on the words that would make me a laughing stock forever. "My BunBun."

"Your what?" At least he had the decency to whisper back.

My cheeks burned. I pulled him behind the canteen. "My stuffed rabbit."

He smirked. For just a second, he got those guppy lips again like he was thinking up some amazingly mean thing to say. Then his face changed like he'd remembered he slept with a nightlight once upon a time. "I didn't take it, Zeke. I didn't even know you had a stuffed animal."

"Like I would tell you." I looked across campus. Anything to keep from looking Kyle in the eyes. "That's why I had to sleep on the top bunk."

"You could have asked."

"Yeah, right. I would have been laughed out of camp."

I waited for him to deny it, but he couldn't. Instead, he asked, "When did you lose it?"

"The night it rained in. I felt you take it."

He denied that. I hadn't expected anything different, and I wasn't disappointed. He blamed the camp thief instead. The one who had been snagging marbles and mirrors and combs and jewelry from the other cabins. He even blamed it on the legendary Camp Crusoe ghost. As if that were possible. Then he finished with a whipped-cream-and-cherry-on-top idea. "I bet the Camp Crusoe thief is nothing but a coon. I bet these woods are full of coon holes with little trinkets from this camp."

It was stupid. What would a raccoon want with a stuffed rabbit? Just in case, though, I had to look. I grabbed Kyle's arm and begged him to help me find BunBun. "I can't go home without it. I can barely sleep now. You have to help me look."

Maybe he thought I was going to hurt him, or maybe he felt sorry for me. Whatever the reason, he agreed to help.

We snuck out after Cabin 13 was asleep. For two hours, we searched trees for coon holes. That might sound easy, but coons are tricky and finding a coon's nest up in a tree was even trickier. We hadn't even found a hint of one yet.

Thunder rumbled. Static sizzled in the air. A zag of lightning streaked across the sky. My eyes stung from the brightness, and for a moment I couldn't see a thing. But I could hear. Somewhere to my left, a branch snapped and Kyle screamed. Another jagged flash and the outline of Kyle hanging from a broken limb shot into view.

He looked so ridiculous, I started to laugh.

"Don't just stand there and laugh. Get me down, you idiot."

The hairs on my scalp bristled. Whatever else I might be, I wasn't stupid. I gritted my teeth until they felt like they would snap off. I threw the worst jab at him I could think of. "At least I can read."

"What does that have to do with anything?" Kyle's voice got all funky, and he sounded like he was ready to cry. Good. At least I wasn't the only one.

If I pushed just a little more, maybe I could get him to finally lay off. "You think I'm here because I'm stupid. You think you can boss me around because you're awesome. Well, guess what? You're not awesome. You can't even read."

The branch cracked again, and Kyle dropped a foot before the branch caught. He hung by one hand. His voice pierced through the air. "I never said you were stupid, but I know I am. Is that better? Is that what you want to hear?"

It was. I had won the summer-long fight. I had broken Kyle. I could walk away now and leave Kyle dangling. My troubles were over. Another bolt of lightning split the sky, and I knew I couldn't leave him hanging in the middle of a storm. I ran over and stood under the tree, stretching my hands up as far as I could. Kyle stepped onto them, and then onto my shoulders. He dropped to the ground. The limb crashed down beside us.

Kyle's voice came out all shaky. "Thank goodness you're so tall."

"Yeah. Thank goodness for thyroid tumors," I mumbled as a clap of thunder nearly knocked us over.

"What's that?"

I pushed away, embarrassed. "Nothing."

He grabbed my arm. "Are you sick?"

"Was. That's what made me grow so fast."

"Not anymore?"

He was like a freakin' bull dog. Maybe I should be glad we weren't friends. His constant nagging would drive me nuts. "I had surgery. It's no big deal."

"Are you okay?"

Seriously, what did he want? More ammunition to start a new fight? Fine. I threw the last grenade in his direction. "Yeah, I'm fine except my medicine makes me wet the bed."

"I didn't know."

"Why would you? It's not like I advertise. My size does that enough."

"I'm glad I know."

I waited for the pity that would make the last two weeks of reading camp even more miserable than the first seven. "Why? So you could feel sorry for me?"

"No. So I could quit feeling sorry for myself. I have dyslexia, and that's why I can't read." Kyle paused. "I can't read. I can't spell. Forget taking tests. Even when I know the stuff I get Fs. That's why I'm here. At least you're just big. I'm a big dummy."

It took a minute for his confession to sink in. All along, I thought I was the only freak. If he felt the same way, maybe he didn't really mean to bully me. Maybe he was just protecting himself from his own embarrassing secret. I dropped my arm around his shoulder. "You're a funny kid, Pipsqueak."

A raindrop splattered on his face. "I think we better get back to camp."

It took everything I had to walk away from those trees. I hadn't slept without my rabbit since my surgery and couldn't imagine leaving camp without her. Not that I had much of a choice. She was missing, and I'd be going home soon. With or without her.

Kyle stopped walking and waited for me to catch up. "I won't tell anyone you sleep with a stuffed rabbit."

I knew he was trying to make me feel better. But more than that, I thought, just maybe, he was trying to be my friend. I tested the waters. "And I won't tell anyone you talk in your sleep."

"Do not," he said.

"Do too."

"Not."

"Too."

Kyle punched me in the shoulder, soft, like friends probably do. "What do I say?"

I almost murmured Sienna's name. Then I thought how I would feel if he teased me about BunBun. I said instead. "You don't want to know. Trust me."

And he did. As strange as that seemed, I think he did.

We ran back to Cabin 13 and snuck in the front door, past Rob to the bunk bed that started it all.

Dear Mom,
I might survive reading camp after all.
Your son,
Ezekial
P.S. My friend Kyle and I figured out who the camp thief was. I'll tell you all about it when Bun Bun and I get home.

Questions

1. At the beginning of camp, Zeke was embarrassed about his stuffed rabbit, so he took the top bunk away from Kyle. What could Zeke have done differently to keep from getting on Kyle's bad side?

2. Zeke thinks Kyle is a bully. If you asked Kyle why might he think Zeke is the bully? Is it possible to be a victim and a bully at the same time? Why or why not?

3. Zeke never talks to his counselor about the problems he has with Kyle, yet Zeke and Kyle somehow work things out. When is it okay to work things out on your own? When does it become necessary to ask an adult for help?

Rosemary's Apples

SARAH TREGAY

MOM HAD DONE IT AGAIN. Like she did every year. She gave Rosemary a bucket of fresh-picked apples to share with her fifth-grade class at Julia Davis Elementary School.

"I got it, Mom," Rosemary said, taking the bucket from the bed of their old pick-up truck.

"Don't forget to tell the class about Tom Davis's apple orchards and how he fed the emigrants on the Oregon Trail," Mom said.

"Yeah, I know."

Mom kissed Rosemary's cheek and then waved goodbye.

Rosemary forced herself to smile. She couldn't wave with the bucket in one hand and her save-the-earth book bag in the other. She didn't really feel like smiling either.

As regular as the seasons, as the buckets of cherries, peaches and apples, Rosemary got teased. Rosemary pressed her lips together in a firm, straight line. She trudged up the walk, hoping the popular kids wouldn't notice her. Or her bucket.

"Poison apples?" Jacob Roberts asked.

"Just in time for Halloween," his sister, Kylie, said. "Mirror, mirror on the wall, who's the fairest of them all?"

"Not Rosemary," Zoë McAlister chimed in. "She's got dirt under her fingernails."

"Back when we were princesses for Halloween, Rosemary was Cinderella," Kylie said. "All chores and no prince charming."

Rosemary ducked her head. *Stupid popular kids,* she thought. What the girls were saying was true. She did have farm chores to do, and she didn't have a boyfriend. When she reached the doors of the school, no one held it open for her. She had to put the bucket down, open the door, and pick it back up again. And for the gazillionth time, Rosemary wished Mom would stop it with the buckets of fruit. They were embarrassing,

In her classroom, Rosemary gave the apples to her teacher, Mrs. Harder. Who, of course, gushed over them. "Oooh, what a treat! Macintosh apples make the best pies. I'll have to get some at the farmer's market on Saturday." Mrs. Harder was a loyal customer at Rosemary's parents' produce stand.

"The best," Rosemary agreed. But her eyes stung a little, as if deep down, she wanted to cry. *Stupid apples,* she thought. *Stupid apples ruined my day.*

Rosemary took her seat. She had the best seat—the one right behind Liam Simon. That made her smile a little bit. From her seat she could look at the back of Liam's neck where the hairs came down to a little point in the middle. He had a birthmark, too. It looked like a lopsided, red heart.

After math next door and science down the hall, the class gathered for English in Mrs. Harder's room. With one hand on the bucket of apples, Mrs. Harder plastered a big smile on her face. "We have a special autumn treat today!"

The class groaned.

Rosemary sank lower in her chair.

"Everyone can have an apple for a mid-morning snack!" Mrs. Harder said.

"They're dirty," Zoë said.

"Yeah, the ones at the store are all shiny," Jacob said.

"That's because the store ones are polished. These are fresh. We can wash and polish these at the sink in the back of the room," Mrs. Harder explained, her smile fading. "Now come up and pick one out."

"I can't," a girl named Marcella whined. "I have braces."

"You're excused," Mrs. Harder said.

Then the class rang with excuses, "I'm allergic." And, "I'm not hungry."

Mrs. Harder wasn't smiling anymore.

And Rosemary had slouched so low in her seat, she had to catch herself from falling onto the floor.

Then Liam raised his hand. "I'll have one."

Mrs. Harder looked relieved.

Liam walked up to the desk and chose a bright red apple. He polished it on his shirt as he walked back to his desk. With a loud snap, he bit into it. Droplets of apple juice sprayed out—one landing on Rosemary's desk.

"Thanks Rosemary," he mumbled through apple bits before he sat down.

Rosemary dipped her finger into the drop of juice, brought it to her nose and inhaled. It smelled sweet and fresh, like the farmer's market. She rubbed the juice into her wrist as if it were expensive perfume.

When the girls at her lunch table turned up their noses at her fried eggplant and tomato sandwich, she sniffed her wrist and looked over their heads to find Liam. When no one picked her for their soccer team in gym class, she smelled her sticky-sweet wrist and thought of Liam. And at the end of the day, when Mrs. Harder asked if she wanted the bucket of apples back, she inhaled the apple scent and thought of Liam.

"No," she said. "I can't take them home again." That stinging feeling pricked her eyes again. "My mom—"

"I understand, dear," Mrs. Harder said. "How about I take them home and bake my husband a pie?"

Rosemary nodded. *At least someone wants my stupid apples.*

"I won't tell your mother," Mrs. Harder said with a wink.

"Okay."

Rosemary held the edges of the plastic grocery sack while Mrs. Harder filled it with apples.

"These smell so good," Mrs. Harder said.

"Yeah," Rosemary agreed. *Like Liam.*

With the bucket empty, Rosemary headed home. She walked through the new subdivision where little trees were starting to turn red. For sale signs hung in several yards. *Four bedrooms,* one read. *Move-in ready,* another announced. Rosemary half wished her family could move into a house here. Rosemary wished her parents worked in an office, wore suits, and ate take-out. Nope. Her parents wore blue jeans, rubber boots, and baseball caps. They worked outside. They ate what grew on the farm: asparagus and rhubarb, strawberries and peas, zucchini and sweet corn, apples and potatoes. She even wished they had named her something besides Rosemary. They grew rosemary in the garden, next to the oregano.

She turned right and walked down the country road where the homes looked as big as hotels. Mom and Daddy said that this used to be farmland just like theirs, with horses on the left hand side and cattle on the right. But Rosemary was little then, and all she could remember was the bang, banging of hammers as the houses were built.

Rosemary shifted the bucket to her other hand. The bucket was empty, but it still felt heavy. Heavy with secrets.

Rosemary found Mom among the rows of tall tomato plants. "How'd your friends like the apples?" Mom asked.

"Okay, I guess," Rosemary said and shrugged. She knew it was a lie. *A little lie,* she told herself. *Because if I tell the truth about Jacob, Kylie and Zoë teasing me, I might cry for real.*

"You need a snack?" Mom asked, nodding her head in the direction of a pile of freshly washed carrots with the tops still on.

Rosemary shook her head.

"Then help me pick. It might freeze tonight."

Rosemary walked down the row and began to work opposite her mother. The tomatoes were as big as softballs, heavy and almost soft under their skins. She picked carefully, not wanting to bruise them. But sometimes a tomato would cling to the vine. Rosemary pulled at a big one. It didn't come free. She used both hands and tugged. Her fingers broke the skin. Pulp, juice and slimy seeds oozed over her grip, trickling down her arms. "Eww!"

"A wormy one?" Mom asked.

Rosemary dropped the tomato and shook the juice from her hands. "No."

Bringing her wrist to her nose, she inhaled. It smelled like V-8. *Not apples. Not Liam.*

And her eyes began to sting. She sank to her haunches and buried her face in her arm. *Stupid tomatoes. Stupid apples. Stupid farm.*

"What's wrong, honey?" Mom asked, stooping beside her.

"The kids at school don't like our apples," Rosemary whispered.

"Oh, they're just used to chips and cookies for snacks."

"No. They like apples," Rosemary said, looking up at Mom. "They don't like *our* apples."

Mom looked hurt. "Why not?"

"Because they aren't shiny. Because they're dirty. Because *I* brought them," Rosemary said through sobs.

"Oh, honey!" Mom said. She hugged Rosemary's shoulders.

"They tease me because I live on a farm. Because I have dirty fingernails and eggplant sandwiches." Rosemary cried.

Mom pulled Rosemary close, rocking her like a baby while she sobbed.

* * *

Later that night, after Daddy got back from delivering a load of pumpkins to the Co-op in Boise, they sat down to dinner. Mom explained that Rosemary had a hard day. But when Rosemary began to tell Daddy about it, her eyes got stingy. She shook her head. Mom told Daddy instead.

"I'm sorry, Sweetie," Daddy said. "I know that it is hard to think about others when you've had a bad day, but I have a feeling that you made Mrs. Harder's day better."

Rosemary nodded. Mrs. Harder was happy. And Liam, too.

After the dishes were done, Mom asked Rosemary if she'd like a manicure.

"What's a manicure?"

"When fancy ladies go to a salon, they get their fingernails done."

"Uh, okay."

Mom got a bowl of warm water, and Rosemary soaked her hands in it. Mom brushed under Rosemary's fingernails with an old toothbrush and then painted them pale blue. Last, Mom rubbed lotion on Rosemary's hands.

"No more Cinderella hands," Rosemary said. *Now I'm ready to hold hands with my prince charming.*

Rosemary walked to school the next day. She took her time hanging up her sweater and putting her lunchbox in her locker in the hall.

"You got any more of those apples?" a voice asked over her shoulder.

"Hi, Liam," she said, surprised that he was talking to her. "No, I—"

"It's okay. Never mind." He turned to go.

Rosemary opened her lunchbox and took out an apple. She held it out to Liam. "Here."

"I don't want to eat your lunch," Liam said, shaking his head.

"I never eat all my lunch anyway."

"Thanks." Liam took the apple, his fingers brushing hers. "Food bank stuff doesn't last all week."

"Oh," Rosemary said. She knew the food bank gave food to people who didn't have enough to eat. Mom and Daddy always donated stuff from the farm.

"My dad lost his job," Liam explained, looking down at the floor. "And I've got two big brothers. They eat lots."

Rosemary nodded. She noticed how Liam's hair formed a little point in the middle of his forehead. "You should come to my house. We've got food coming out our ears!"

Liam laughed at her joke and took a bite of her apple.

They walked to the classroom and took their seats.

Rosemary looked at the back of Liam's neck. His head bobbed as he munched the apple down to the core. And the lopsided-heart birthmark looked a bit like an apple.

After school, Rosemary found Mom in the kitchen canning tomatoes. Steam rose up from the pots on the stove.

"The girls at my lunch table liked my nail polish," she announced. "And they didn't even know that the jelly on my P.B.J was homemade."

"That's nice, Honey," Mom said. "You need a snack?"

Rosemary nodded, and Mom sliced a red tomato and sprinkled it with sugar. Rosemary sat and ate.

Then the doorbell rang. Rosemary popped the last slice in her mouth and ran to answer it. On her porch steps stood Liam.

"Hi!" Rosemary squeaked when her breath caught.

"Hi," he said with a big grin. "You said to come over. So here I am!"

Mom came into the foyer drying her hands, and Rosemary made introductions."So nice to meet you," Mom said. "Maybe Rosemary can show you around."

Rosemary didn't think that was a good idea. She hadn't exactly made her bed this morning. She asked instead, "You want to see the garden?"

Liam nodded.

Rosemary winced. *Who ever heard of a princess giving Prince Charming a tour of a vegetable garden?* Reluctantly, she led the way around the house. *This is a stupid idea,* she thought. Then, stepping over a pile of discarded rhubarb leaves, she announced, "This is the garden."

"Wow!" Liam looked around. "It's huge."

He's impressed? "It's about half an acre—not including the pumpkins."

Liam wandered down the main path, and Rosemary pointed out the different plants. "These are raspberries, and these are the strawberries. There's no fruit now. They're summer plants."

Liam soaked the information in like he was soaking in the sun.

"Tomatoes are fall things," Rosemary continued. "These are Sweet-100s." She plucked a cherry tomato from the vine and handed it to Liam.

He bit it, and his face brightened.

That instant Rosemary's negative thoughts floated away. She slid a tomato into her mouth, and the flavor burst over her tongue.

Then she continued her tour, happily picking bits of herbs and yellow wax beans for Liam to try as they went.

"I still think the apples are my favorite," he said, chewing on a carrot that they had dug up and washed under the garden hose.

"Want to pick some?"

"That'd be cool."

Rosemary found a bucket but didn't bother with a ladder. In the orchard, she showed Liam the oldest tree. It was the best for climbing because it had a series of evenly spaced branches and the first one was easy to reach.

He scaled it like a pro, placing his sneakers in the Vs until he was surrounded by green leaves and red apples.

Rosemary climbed up after him.

A breeze rustled the leaves around them, drowning out other sounds. They were alone under a canopy of apples and leaves. They picked an apple each and polished them on their shirts.

"I like your birthmark," Rosemary said. "It looks like a heart, or an apple. I can't decide."

"Thanks," Liam said. "I like your farm."

"You do?" Rosemary bit into her apple.

"Yeah. You can walk outside and get anything you want to eat."

"Not ice cream and cookies," Rosemary said.

"At my house you can see the back of the fridge. And

if there were cookies, my brothers would eat them all."

"Maybe you can take some stuff home with you," Rosemary offered.

"Yeah. My own stash of apples," Liam said, sounding as if he were talking more to himself than to Rosemary.

"You sure like apples."

"I like your apples best," Liam said, taking a big bite of the one in his hand. "Jacob, Zoë and Kylie don't know what they're talking about."

"Yes they do. Their new subdivisions *are* nicer than our old farm."

"No they're not. I live there, too. The houses are all beige, the fences are plastic, and the trees are so little you can't climb them."

Rosemary laughed. Liam made the subdivisions sound kind of silly.

"Besides, without your farm we wouldn't have these." He held up his apple. "Or..." he trailed off.

"Or what?" Rosemary asked.

Liam bit his lip and his ears turned pink. "Or us."

"Yeah," she agreed with a smile. Rosemary thought about yesterday and how the popular kids had teased her about the very same apples. They had made her cry. Now she was sitting in an apple tree with Liam Simon—and she could already tell that he was a better friend than any of them would ever be. She reached to pick an apple and placed it in the bucket for Liam to take home.

Questions

1. Rosemary's neighborhood in Idaho used to have many farms, but now it is a mix of new subdivisions and her parents' farm. Is this good or bad? How come?

2. William's family has hit hard times while others in the community, like Rosemary's family, donate food to those in need. Have you ever donated to a food bank or charity? How did it feel to help others? How would it feel to be helped if you needed it?

3. William befriends Rosemary even though the "popular kids" bully her. Have you ever made a new friend despite what others think? If you were bullied, would having a friend make you feel better or worse?

4. The fairy tale *Cinderella* is referenced in "Rosemary's Apples." Rosemary is bullied in this story. Was Cinderella bullied? Do you think bullying is something new or something old?

One Above Zero

K.R. SMITH

ZOE WATCHED THE TOES of her small, white sneakers peek out in turn past the books clutched tightly to her chest. She hurried through the hallway to her class. Looking neither left nor right, she avoided the faces of those who stared, or worse, laughed. That laughter would be more than she could bear today. No matter how fast her thin legs tried to go, however, she couldn't outrun the whispers. As she entered the classroom and slipped into her desk chair, the hisses began from those seated behind her, punctuated by her name.

Mr. Clayton, the math teacher, closed the door and said, "Okay, class, open your books to section five. That's on page eighty-seven, I believe."

A collective moan filled the room in protest. The time for socializing was over.

"I see you're all anxious to get started," Mr. Clayton said.

"Do we really have to learn all this?" asked a boy sitting in the back of the classroom.

"It would be a very good idea for you to do so," Mr. Clayton replied with a deep sigh. "Mathematics is one of the basic tools you'll need to master other subjects and have a better understanding of the world around you."

"This stuff?"

"Here's a really simple example. Let's say you're designing a car to carry a maximum of eight hundred pounds. Using division, you can determine it can carry four or five people, so you'll need four or five seats. With six seats, you could go over the rated capacity if six average-sized people sat in it at the same time. Of course, to fully design a car, you'll need a whole lot more—like geometry, trigonometry, and calculus, but that all builds on what we're learning here today."

"Just put Zoe in it and you could probably fit seven people, and you wouldn't need calculus," said Kyle, hiding behind his book. When he heard the others laugh, he added, "Her weight is like a negative number."

Then Brad chimed in, "And you'd still have plenty of room."

"That's enough. We don't need any class clowns," Mr. Clayton remarked.

"Just put her in the trunk," one of the girls said.

"Okay, class, let's end that right now and get back to the lesson."

Although the comments ceased, the stares and the stifled laughs remained. Zoe tried not to look at anyone, but she wasn't paying much attention to her work, either.

Her stomach churned as she clenched her teeth to keep from crying. All she could think of was getting out of that room. Once the bell rang, Zoe rushed through the door, eager to be anywhere else. It was only the first half of her day, and it had started like so many others—listening to the whispers, the rumors, and the jokes—all at her expense. She had no reason to believe the rest of the day would be any better.

She was next to her locker when Brad passed by on the way to the cafeteria. He stopped and watched her for a moment as she struggled with the lock, finally giving up and resting her head against the locker. When Brad walked up behind Zoe, it startled her, and she spun around to face him.

"They wouldn't laugh if you weren't so skinny," Brad said. "Why don't you eat more? You know, like a couple of burgers for lunch."

Zoe turned away from Brad, her head bowed to hide the tear running down her face.

"I do eat," she replied while wiping her face. "I eat all the time. And I take medicine all the time. But it only helps a little and everyone still laughs."

"Medicine? You mean, like you're sick or something?"

"Sort of."

"Oh." Brad backed up a step.

"Don't worry. You can't catch it. It's my thyroid. It doesn't work right."

"Thyroid? I—I didn't know. I'm not even sure what a thyroid is. Is that bad?"

"What does it matter? I'm just a big nothing to you— and everyone. Maybe less than nothing. I'm a negative number, remember?"

"Look, I was just teasing..."

"Yeah, teasing. It's always just teasing. But it's all the time. Except when you want to make a joke. Then you just laugh out loud. Why do you hate me so much?"

Zoe turned and ran down the hall away from Brad.

He watched until she rounded the corner, the sound of her footsteps growing fainter until they disappeared.

"I don't hate you," he replied, but there was no one left to hear.

The conversation lingered in Brad's thoughts, disturbed by the notion that what he considered a joke had hurt someone. He didn't understand Zoe's problem or why she just couldn't eat more to put on weight. He had noticed her hair was thin, and she had always been skinny, but he never knew she was actually sick.

On his way to lunch, he took a detour into the library. He thought it might have some books about Zoe's condition. When the librarian was alone, Brad went up to her and asked, "Do you have any books on thyroids?"

"I assume you mean the thyroid? It's an organ of the human body, not a bunch of space aliens in a video game."

"Yeah. I guess."

"Is there something in particular you would like to know about it? Where it's located or what it looks like?"

"I'm not sure. Just anything about them—or it, I mean."

The librarian searched "thyroid" on her computer and printed a list of books in the library. It was not a long one. She led Brad across the room to the shelves were the few medical books the library held were kept.

"We don't have much. Perhaps when you have a better

idea of what you need, you can do a search on the Internet for medical sites with more information."

Brad took the books to a table and opened the first one. There were pictures showing the thyroid and how it was located at the base of the neck. It looked like two small blobs on each side of the throat. He felt his own neck, but wasn't sure he had found anything that could be his thyroid. Below the pictures was a description of how it controlled the body's metabolism. There was also a list of symptoms for an overactive thyroid. Brad whispered each one as he followed his finger down the list: nervousness, tiredness, weight loss, and hair loss. Brad continued until he came across the section on treatment and found that what Zoe had told him was true. He kept reading until there was nothing more to read, closed the books, and sat silently for a while as he stared out the window. He could see children outside on the playground. They were healthy, strong, and growing, while Zoe, at the mercy of this tiny organ, was weak and frail. He learned a lot more in that library than what was on those printed pages.

After lunch the following day, Brad waited for Zoe near her locker knowing she would need to get books for the second half of the day. He knew it wouldn't be easy to talk to her, and he paced as he tried to figure out what to say. When she did arrive, Zoe went straight past him to her locker as if he wasn't there.

Brad licked his dry lips, then went up to her and said, "Hi."

Zoe glanced up at Brad without saying a word, and then went back to what she was doing.

"Zoe," Brad said, swallowing hard, "I was thinking about what you told me—you know, about being sick—and

I found some books about thyroids in the library. It was like you said—how the medicine doesn't always help." Brad watched Zoe for a moment, waiting for her to respond. When she didn't, he added, "I read you might even need an operation."

Zoe turned enough to look at Brad, but not directly. "Well, I don't have to do that. At least not yet."

"I didn't know it was that bad. Do you get scared?"

"Sometimes," Zoe replied. She fumbled with her books for a moment, and then said, "I have to go to class now."

Brad stepped back as Zoe turned to leave. Before taking a full step, however, she saw that a group of kids had filled the hall a couple of classrooms away, almost blocking it. A few were watching her and laughing. Zoe stopped, and with her eyes still on the group, took a step back.

"What's wrong?" Brad asked.

"They're just waiting for me to come by so they can have another laugh or push me around. I can go outside and come back in by the gym to get to class."

"But you're not going to. This is the shortest way," Brad said, pointing up the hall. "Come on."

"I can't..."

"You can if you're not by yourself."

"I'm always by myself."

"No, you're not. You're with someone right now."

"Do you mean—with you?" Zoe asked.

"Yeah," Brad nodded. "With me."

"They'll just laugh at you, too."

"Maybe." He remembered how the kids taunted anyone who tried to be Zoe's friend. "But maybe they won't laugh so hard this time."

Zoe felt just a hint of courage somewhere inside, but still hesitated.

"It's okay," Brad said. He held out his hand for her. "Come on."

She looked into his eyes, then took it and began to walk with him. Zoe wondered why he was doing this, but was relieved that he was with her. She felt strength growing within knowing she was no longer alone. As Brad pulled Zoe along behind, her grip tightened with each step. As they got nearer to the kids, a couple of the boys started to grin.

"Hey, Brad! What are you doing? Taking your dog for a walk?"

"Just get out of the way, Kyle."

"I don't need to," he said laughing. "She can squeeze through anywhere."

Brad turned to Kyle and asked, "Is something funny?"

"I don't know. Maybe there is," Kyle shrugged.

Brad, in a serious tone, said, "No, there isn't. Leave her alone, Kyle. She isn't bothering you. Or anyone."

As a voice from the back of the group timidly agreed, a few of the kids moved away from Kyle, leaving him to face Brad alone.

Looking over his shoulder, Kyle asked, "Where's everybody going?"

"It's almost time for class," a girl replied.

"Yeah. Let's go," another added.

When Brad edged forward, Kyle stumbled backward into the lockers and dropped his notebook. It burst into an avalanche of white paper across the floor. Brad and Zoe stepped by as a Kyle, on his hands and knees, shoveled up his schoolwork.

As the two walked down the hall together, it was the first time ever that Zoe felt like part of the class, or perhaps anything. She turned and looked back at the group. They seemed less frightening somehow. Then she looked up at Brad who returned her glance with a smile. No, not everyone understood, but sometimes it's enough that somebody does, even if it's only one. After all, anything above zero is a positive number.

Questions

1. Has anyone teased or bullied you because of your appearance? How did that make you feel?

2. Why do you think Kyle picked on Zoe instead of some other student?

3. Brad had to stand up to a group of students to help Zoe. Why is that difficult to do?

4. Do you think it will be easier for the kids to accept Zoe now that Brad is her friend?

5. What are some other ways to help someone in a situation like this?

The Popcorn Tree

CAT WOODS

I PEERED INTO MY LUNCH BOX, past the mandarin oranges and the peanut butter and banana sandwich. I honed in on my favorite snack in the whole world. Popcorn. I unzipped the plastic baggie and scooped up a handful.

To my left, Janna scrunched her nose. "How can you eat that stuff, Katy? If it's not a popcorn ball, no thank you."

I shrugged and popped a half-soggy kernel into my mouth. Butter exploded and salt tickled my tongue. "I like it this way."

To my right, Harper let out a sigh of longing. "Cold is the only way I get popcorn."

Practically perfect Janna snorted juice out her nose. "Don't they have microwaves in the trailer park?"

Everyone at the table laughed. Everyone except Harper and me. I stared straight ahead and popped another kernel into my mouth. This time it tasted like cardboard. I hated that my two best friends couldn't stand each other. It wasn't Harper's fault that her clothes were hand-me-downs or that the only treats she got were leftovers from her dad's job at the movie theater.

Janna dabbed at the orange drink on the hem of her white sweater dress. Within the week she would get a new shirt to replace the ruined one. She looked up from the barely stained spot. "I wanted a different color anyway."

"I'd pick blue," Harper said dreamily. She always picked blue. It was her favorite color.

"Exactly why I wouldn't," Janna said and let her eyes wander over Harper's rumpled t-shirt and faded blue jeans.

My stomach pinched tight, squeezing away my appetite. Beside me, Harper's stomach growled. I knew peanut butter and banana sandwiches were her favorite, but I didn't offer up my uneaten lunch. I didn't want Janna to call Harper a moocher and make her feel bad in front of the entire fifth grade class.

That night, I made a wish on a shooting star.

When I awoke, I found a small packet of seeds on my pillow. The fancy writing spelled out directions.

Today at noon in the shade of a tree,
dig a hole and plant some seeds.
Walk three times in a circle clock-wise.
Make a wish before the crow flies.

My hand shook as I tucked the packet of seeds into my lunch box. I didn't really believe in magic, but there was no other explanation for the note. Besides, I would try anything to get my friends to like each other.

All the way to school, I considered the best place to plant the seeds. I had no idea what would grow from them or what kind of spell I should say. I wished there had been more directions, but the backside of the envelope was empty.

The playground was not. I dropped my backpack on the cement outside the school doors and searched the crowd. Loud cheering drew me to the swing set. Harper stood in the middle of the group. The pocket of her blue sweatshirt was ripped, and her pig tails had come undone.

Janna pushed her face right up to Harper's. "Yeah, well you stink like a pig barn. Why don't you go back to the farm where you belong?"

The crowd cheered.

Tears ran down Harper's face. She swiped at them with dirty hands, leaving a smudge on her cheeks. My heart pounded in my chest. How could Janna say something like that?

Harper's eyes locked on mine. For just a second, they lit up, as if they were asking for help. I wanted to help her. I wanted to save Harper, but I didn't want to lose Janna's friendship in the process.

Not knowing what to do, I looked away.

Harper's scream ripped through the air. "I don't even need you. I don't need any of you."

The playground guards descended on the scene. One put an arm around Harper. The other shook her finger at Janna. I knew it wouldn't do any good. It never did. Right then and there, I silently vowed to share my sandwich with Harper at lunch. That would make her feel better.

But all morning, Harper avoided me. At lunch, she didn't sit at my table. She sat alone. Janna gave me a wrapped package. It was the white sweater. Yesterday, I would have squealed and held the dress up to my chin. Today, I felt like throwing it in the trash.

I looked up from my unwanted gift. Janna's bottom lip quivered. "I got another white one so we can be twins."

The twin thing started the time we went to the zoo. We'd both pulled our dark hair back into smooth ponytails and put on matching shirts. All day long, people smiled and whispered about how adorable identical twins were. Mostly, I liked being Janna's twin. After this morning, though, the thought made my stomach hurt. I forced a smile. "Thanks."

As soon as we were dismissed for recess, I grabbed the packet of seeds. I headed to the far corner of the playground where the tennis courts lined one side and a bunch of trees closed in on the other.

I ducked behind the pines to a little clearing. This place was off limits and would earn me an hour in the principal's office if I got caught. My seeds should have plenty of privacy to grow here.

A giant crow opened its yellow beak and cawed from an overhead branch. It sounded like he said, "Warning. Warning."

A shiver spread down my back like a dribble of ice water. I didn't have time to think about warnings. I had to do something before the crow flew away and my best friends became my worst enemies. Just once, I wanted Harper to have something nice. Then maybe Janna would be nice to her.

At noon exactly, I scooped the dirt away and ripped open the packet. Rainbow colored popcorn seeds spilled into my palm. I dropped them into the hole, covered them up, and walked around the mound three times.

As I walked, I chanted. "Ring around the popcorn seeds, hoping for a friendship tree. Give my friend treats galore, so Janna won't tease her anymore. Ring around the popcorn seeds, friends forever we shall be."

I wanted nothing more in the whole world than for my friends to be friends. I wanted us all to get along. But when nobody showed up after school for the walk home, I worried that my friends didn't even like me anymore. It didn't make sense. I hadn't done anything. I was nice to both of them. If that spell didn't hurry up and work, I was going to be the loneliest girl in the whole school.

The next morning, I left for school early and snuck into the clearing. It smelled like a giant popcorn bowl. A new tree grew where the mound had been. Steaming popcorn hung from its branches.

"Magic is real!" I sang to the crow.

He bobbed his head and squawked, "Warning. Warning."

I shooed him away and plucked a few kernels from the tree. I dropped them into my lunch box. I found Harper tucked inside a tube slide on the baby section of the playground. It's where she always went when she was mad. I crawled up the slide until I clung to the plastic just below her feet.

Unsure of what to say, I imitated Harper's favorite radio announcer. "So, I had a funny dream the other night."

I waited for her to ask about it, but the only sound was the wind whistling past the opening of the slide. I clutched my windbreaker close, even though it wasn't the spring air that gave me a chill.

Harper's voice came out sharp. "I don't even know why you like Janna. She's a spoiled brat. And a bully."

I knew Harper was right. But Janna was my friend. She was nice to me and fun to be around. But Harper would never understand that, just like Janna didn't even try to see anything good about Harper. For a second I envied them both. At least they weren't in the middle of two friends who hated each other. And really, wasn't Harper being just as mean by calling Janna names?

Harper shifted. In the semi-darkness, the charms attached to her shoe laces glowed a pale blue. B-F-F. For us, the initials meant Best Film Friends. The matching set was on my shoes. A gift from Harper, they had been my favorite birthday present last year, and were a constant reminder of the times we'd spent the night in the theater acting like famous film critics while her dad cleaned up.

Even though Janna was my twin, Harper was still my best friend. Somehow, I had to let her know that. "I'm sorry about yesterday. Janna doesn't always think before she says things."

"Well, she should," Harper said with a sniffle.

I agreed. I also knew that Janna said lots of good things, too. But Janna wasn't here right now, and Harper was. I needed to fix our friendship first and worry about Janna later. "Are you still mad at me?"

Harper sighed. It was a long, hollow sound in the shadows of the tube. "Not angry. Just sad."

I didn't like the thought of that. When Harper got sad, she failed her spelling tests and didn't get her homework done. She also quit eating. I fished the popcorn from my lunchbox. "I have something for you."

The smell of fresh popped corn filled the air. Harper took the kernels from my outstretched hand and dropped them into her mouth. "Oh, my gosh. They're still warm. How did you keep them warm? And the butter. It tastes so real I could cry."

"Don't cry, Harper. It was supposed to make you happy."

"I am happy."

"Good," I said. "Now let's get out of here, and I'll show you your very own popcorn tree."

I dragged Harper to the clearing. A second tree grew beside the first. Harper plucked the plump kernels from the branches and shoveled them in her mouth. "Did you taste this? It's crisp and crunchy and absolutely amazing."

But I wasn't amazed. I was worried. I'd asked for one tree, but now there were two. The only thing that had changed was me telling Harper.

I grabbed her hands. "No matter what, you can't tell anyone about these trees. Not a single soul."

We twisted pinkies to make a promise. The trees were our secret. Feeling better, I plucked some popcorn from the new tree. It was cold and chewy just how I liked it. We ate until the bell rang, calling us in to class.

We were still so full at lunch neither of us ate a bite.

After school, we stuffed our tummies with more delicious popcorn. We overstuffed them. My stomach hurt so much, I barely made it to school the next day. Even so, I felt the pull of the clearing like it was a giant magnet. I ate and ate and ate. Harper joined me.

"I've had enough popcorn," she said between bites and rubbed her bulging belly. Yet, at recess we were once again pulled in the direction of the popcorn trees.

I wanted to cry. The line in my spell about eating treats galore niggled at my brain. It seemed that as long as the trees existed, we could only eat popcorn. With dread, I parted the pine branches and entered the clearing.

Harper groaned. A third tree arched gracefully beside the other two. This one had blue tinted popcorn balls hanging where leaves should have been. The only person I knew who ate blue popcorn balls was Janna.

I glared at Harper. "You pinky swore."

She flinched. "I only told Janna to make her jealous."

"Obviously it didn't work, or she'd be here right now, eating herself sick like us. She probably didn't even believe you. I mean, who would?"

Harper's face sagged.

I realized what I had said. Without thinking, I'd sounded just like Janna and hurt my best friend's feelings. "Not because you aren't trustworthy. Just because she doesn't like you. Not to mention, a popcorn tree is kind of unbelievable."

The strong scent of caramel filled the air, followed by cheddar. Two more saplings pushed through the dirt. Their branches stretched and tangled. Fallen popcorn littered the ground.

My guts churned. Something had definitely gone wrong with my magic spell. First the endless eating, and now a new tree growing for every person who was told. I imagined Janna making fun of Harper's popcorn tree claim to a bunch of kids. I had to stop her now…and somehow break the spell in the process.

I stepped through the line of trees and scanned the school yard. Janna stood among a crowd, laughing and talking. Others made their way toward the group. I sprinted to them, determined to stop the spread of the trees.

Janna made a face. "Can you believe she said that?"

I pushed through the group to stand in front of her. "Knock it off."

"Knock what off? Your little friend is a liar."

"Harper's not…," I stopped and looked around. Sixteen kids now surrounded us. If I said anything about the trees, a dozen more would grow. My stomach hurt just thinking about it. My magic was nothing but a curse. Just like my broken friendships.

Janna snorted. "She's not what? Your friend? Just go ahead and say it. You'll feel better when you do. Then you can join me without your trailer park pal."

Fine. If Janna wanted to end it right here, I would. "Harper is not any of the things you say about her. She's kind and funny and generous."

Janna's laugh cut through the air. "Generous? What does she share with you, Katy? You're poorer just for hanging around her."

Poor.

The word hit me hard. Had I wanted Harper to be rich? Did I think never-ending popcorn would make Janna like Harper? I'd been an idiot. I liked my friends for who they were, not for what they had. But sometimes, I didn't like them at all. Not when they were mean.

I took a deep breath. "Harper spends time with me and makes me laugh. I like who I am when I'm with her. I also like who I am when I'm with you. But from now on, I'm not going to let either of you talk bad about each other. Every time you do, nasty feelings grow. It's like you plant these seeds of hate and once they bloom, you get so full that it almost chokes you. You can't think of anything else. It's like…it's like those butter-blasted popcorn trees."

"They're real?" Janna's eyes flashed with disbelief.

I nodded. "Come on, I'll show you."

But when we broke through the clearing, only one popcorn tree remained. Its branches hung with mouth-watering popcorn of all kinds. Cheddar, buffalo chicken, sweet and salty, and caramel, to name a few.

Harper jumped up and down. "I don't know what you did, but I think you broke the curse. All of a sudden, the trees withered up and disappeared. This is all that's left of an entire popcorn forest."

"I think it's perfect." I admired the odd little tree with a flavor for everyone. Janna picked a blue popcorn ball and held it out to Harper. "I'm sorry. I just got so jealous when Katy spent time with you. I was afraid of losing her."

"I felt the same way," Harper said and accepted Janna's gift.

I bear-hugged my besties. "You're not losing a friend, silly. You're gaining a new one."

Questions

1. It is easy to judge people by the way they look or by the clothes they wear. Janna doesn't like Harper for a silly reason. What is it? What are some other reasons we treat people differently? Why is this unfair?

2. Katy is in a difficult situation because her two best friends don't get along. Is it possible to be friends with people who dislike each other, or is it better only to have friends who get along? What would be hard about each of those situations?

3. What is the definition of a true friend?

4. What do the popcorn trees represent in this story?

Two Heads Are Better Than One

LINDA BREWER

JOEY PEEKED AROUND THE TREE and spied Emmy walking by herself down the snowy sidewalk. Good! He was afraid he had missed her. She was later than usual, and several other kids had already been by. He ducked back so she wouldn't see him.

His mother used to take care of her before and after school, but when Emmy had started third grade this year, her mom had decided that she was big enough to be alone for a few hours. It was easy to keep an eye out for her because the middle school got out earlier than the elementary school.

She looked so little… Pipsqueak! His lips curled in a sneer as he heard her footsteps coming closer. Her boots squeaked and crunched in the snow, and with every step he felt a thrill mount in his chest as he prepared to leap out at her. He hated those stupid pink boots with the fur tops that she always wore. He grinned, knowing that she would probably start crying when he knocked her down again. What a baby!

His mom was always saying how cute Emmy was and how smart Emmy was—Emmy, Emmy, Emmy! He was tired of hearing about it. He thought she looked like a troll doll, and she was really so dumb that she didn't even change her route to avoid him. She'd started walking with a friend sometimes, but the friend wasn't much bigger than she was. Those days, though, he left her alone because he figured her friend would probably tattle. Emmy never told because he'd threatened to hurt her cat if she did.

She was only a few feet away when he sprang out in front of her and she stopped, eyes wide like she was somehow surprised, even though this was like the fiftieth time he'd done it. Idiot.

"Hi, Pipsqueak!" he taunted. "Ready for your daily freeze?"

She just stood there, staring.

He snickered at all the layers of scarves she was bundled in, topped by a silly panda hat. If it weren't for those stupid boots, he wouldn't even be able to tell who it was. "You look like you were attacked by a closet!" His laugh echoed through the quiet of the falling snow.

She didn't reply, and his eyes narrowed. Usually she had started to run by this time, and he liked to chase her for a minute or two before he plowed her down into a drift.

"Cat got your tongue, Pipsqueak?" he tried again.

Her breathing quickened, puffs of steam escaping from the scarves wrapped around her head, but she didn't budge.

This was getting ridiculous. He reached out and gave her a little shove to get her started.

"Whaaa?" he gasped as one mittened hand shot forward and grabbed his wrist, then tugged sharply as the other pushed hard on his chest. He lost his balance when he felt her boot hook his ankle, and then landed face down in the snow with his arm pulled behind him.

"Oof," he gasped as she dropped her full weight on top of him and pushed his arm up his back like a chicken wing. She was a lot heavier than she looked! He thrashed his head back and forth and tried to shift her off by rocking his body. The ice and snow started getting up his nose and into his mouth, and he started to cough. She inched up to his shoulders and pinned him so that he couldn't move without getting more snow in his mouth. He felt like he could hardly breathe. Tears filled his eyes.

He stopped struggling and she leaned forward. "Don't bother me again," she growled softly into his ear, then pushed his face back into the snow as she got up. She brushed herself off and ran lightly across the yards to her house, pulled the key up from the string around her neck, used it to open the front door, then quickly went inside.

Joey slowly pushed himself up and got to his knees. He wiped his face on his coat sleeve and an icy trickle of snow ran down to his elbow. Afraid that someone might have seen, he hurried down the street to his own house. When had Emmy learned Karate?

Had he looked through her front window as he passed, he would have been surprised to see not one little girl, but two—with big grins on their faces, giving each other high fives and trading snow boots.

"I don't think he'll bother you any more, Emmy," said Grace. "He thinks you can defend yourself like a blue belt!"

"I wish I'd seen his face!" Emmy crowed.

"Good thing he didn't see mine!" Grace laughed. "Ready to go to Tae Kwon Do?"

Emmy carefully folded her new white belt and uniform into her backpack, and the girls left the house together arm in arm.

"You're going to tell your mom now, right?" asked Grace.

"Yes," said Emmy, "I promised you I would. I just didn't want to make her worry about me being at home by myself. Now that you've taken care of things, I think he'll stay away."

They passed the Joey-shaped snow angel near the tree. "Thanks for helping me, Grace," said Emmy.

"No problem," said Grace. "That's what friends are for."

Questions

1. Some people think that being disrespectful or rude to someone they don't like is okay. They may even feel like the person deserves it. Why does Joey dislike Emmy? Is it a good reason? Have you ever been rude to someone and thought it was okay because you had a good reason?

2. Bullying is hurting someone on the inside or the outside. How does Joey hurt Emmy on the inside? How does he hurt her on the outside? Which one would be worse?

3. Even though Joey doesn't like Emmy, what could he have done differently? What are some ways you can treat people you don't like? Which behaviors are acceptable? Which ones are not?

4. Emmy took care of her problems by herself. What is the difference between standing up for yourself and fighting back?

Emergency Exit

EDEN GREY

JOSEPHINE HAD BEEN ALIVE for exactly 96,423 hours at 3:25 p.m. That was the precise time she was born eleven years ago. It was a very important day.

"Wait right here! We'll be back after practice," Skylar said.

"With your birthday surprise," Ashley added with a big smile.

The girls skipped off, arm-in-arm. They were the stars of the sixth-grade volleyball team.

Josephine was the star of nothing.

With her spiky, black hair and daily uniform of sweats and Crocs, Josephine was not pretty. Not like Skylar and Ashley. Her grades were average, and she didn't qualify for the spelling bee. She was a failure at absolutely every sport ever invented. She couldn't sing or play an instrument, and she would certainly be too clumsy to try out for the school play.

Josephine had Asperger's Syndrome. She preferred words and numbers to people.

"Hello, Josie," Mrs. Harcourt said as she walked by. Her long skirts swished around her legs, making a sound like waves on a sandy beach.

Josephine wondered if it would make the same sound if *she* wore a long skirt. Definitely not. She was more likely to trip over the fabric than take long, graceful steps in it.

"I said, *Hello, Josie,*" the school secretary repeated.

Josephine looked at Mrs. Harcourt. Why did some people always call her *Josie* instead of her full name? Josephine Marie Clements actually liked her own name a lot. She wanted to say something, but she'd learned her lesson the last time she corrected Mrs. Harcourt. She didn't want to sit through in-school detention ever again.

So Josephine said nothing, but she smiled. It wasn't easy, and she had to bite the tip of her tongue while she did it. Josephine's teacher, Mr. Kellers, knew that Josephine wasn't the kind of girl to chit-chat, but he had taught her that smiles often took the place of words. It seemed to work this time.

Mrs. Harcourt let out a long breath and swished away.

Josephine settled on top of her puffy winter coat to wait. She was tucked into the nook between a big, clunky heat vent box-thing and the emergency exit door at the end of the sixth-grade hall. The gymnasium where Skylar and Ashley were practicing volleyball was down the hall, around a corner, down the combined fourth- and fifth-grade hall, and then past the lobby. It was exactly 380 Josephine-sized steps from the emergency doors to the gymnasium entrance. These steps were in the opposite direction she normally walked after school.

Earlier that day, the entire class had sung "Happy Birthday," and Josephine passed out her mother's handmade invitations to her birthday party this Saturday. Skylar and Ashley said they couldn't come because they had a volleyball game, but they had a surprise for her today if she would wait. Right then, Josephine had felt happy.

The girls said Josephine would get her surprise after they were done with volleyball practice. That meant Josephine had to stay after school for an extra hour. It was very difficult to break her routine, even for a surprise gift.

Every day, Josephine left school at 3:35 and walked straight home. Then she had a snack and did homework until 5:15, when her mother got home. Then she helped with dinner, ate dinner, and helped clean up. After that Josephine and her mother read or watched TV or played games on the Wii.

Today was different. Josephine would wait here until 4:35, then get her birthday surprise from Skylar and Ashley, and then walk home. She expected to be home by 4:55, when she could do a little homework and then help her mother with dinner. It would be mostly like any other day, just with a surprise wait and a surprise gift as a reward.

While waiting, Josephine counted the big cream-colored bricks on the opposite wall; 124 between classrooms. Then the ceiling tiles; 355 in this hallway. She counted doorways, window panes, fliers, posters, and cobwebs. She counted doorknobs and hinges, floor tiles, and black rubber shoe-marks.

It was 3:48 when Josephine ran out of things to count. She pulled out her math homework to stay busy. The predictability of numbers calmed her nerves.

At 4:34 Josephine closed her books and put them away inside her backpack. The squeaking and squealing of tennis shoes echoed from the gymnasium.

A strange, tingly feeling tickled in Josephine's stomach. She smiled, even though no one was around to see it. She forced the feeling down and continued to wait.

When her watch ticked over from 4:44 to 4:45 Josephine wasn't smiling anymore.

At 5:30 she was still waiting.

At 6:15 Josephine heard the familiar swish-swish, like waves. She snuggled deeper into her jacket, afraid of getting in trouble. Mrs. Harcourt appeared in the dark hallway. She gasped, pressed one hand to her mouth and scrunched down close to Josephine.

"Josie! What are you doing here?"

Josephine squeezed her hands together, her nails shining a ghostly hue against her pale fingers in the dull glow from the emergency exit light.

Mrs. Harcourt gently took Josephine's hand and led her to the principal's office, 219 dizzy steps away.

Josephine's mother was waiting there. She scooped her daughter up in her arms and looked her over, as if searching for cuts or bruises. "Honey, are you okay? Did anyone hurt you? I was so worried about you!"

"Mom? What are you doing here? Is Skylar with you?"

"What? No, honey, Skylar isn't here. School's over, everyone went home."

"Are you sure? What about Ashley? I didn't get my

birthday present yet. They had a surprise for my birthday, but I had to wait until after volleyball practice," Josephine explained. Her voice sounded as flat and as empty as she felt. "I waited, just like they said. Did they come with you?"

"Oh, Josephine, honey," was all her mother said.

Josephine deduced two things from those three little words. First, that Skylar and Ashley were not here. Second, that there was no surprise, no gift, no special moment for her special birthday. They had tricked her. Skylar and Ashley were not her friends. Josephine was not a special girl.

She cried then, sobbing into her mother's hair.

Josephine and her mother went home and ordered Chinese take-out. Josephine didn't have to do her homework or help clean up. For dessert they made a double chocolate cake and ate it until they felt a little sick. Then they watched *Spirited Away*, Josephine's favorite movie, and they talked.

They talked about what friends are like, and what friends are not like.

Friends do not lie to you. They do not promise you gifts and then leave you all alone. Friends do not play tricks on you. They do not take advantage of you or laugh behind your back.

That night Josephine dreamed of being locked in the school, alone, with no coat and no backpack. It was so cold, and very dark. In the dream, Josephine found her nook by the heater in the sixth-grade hall and made herself comfortable in the light of the emergency exit.

She listened for the telltale sound of waves washing up on a lonely beach.

Questions

1. How was Josephine tricked? Have you ever been tricked by friends?

2. Do you know someone with Asperger's Syndrome? How is he/she different than you? How are you two the same?

3. If someone you know had a bad birthday, what could you do to make it better?

Blindsided

LAUREN NEIL

JACK'S MOM WAS ON A MISSION, and he was slowing her down. On purpose, of course. "Come on, Jack, hurry up." She bustled around the front door and quickly grabbed her purse, keys, and sunglasses.

"Where are we going," Jack asked, as he dragged his feet toward the door. He knew they were going to the mall; his mom had told him about a million times. He also knew that it bugged her when he asked the same question over and over.

She took a deep breath. "The mall. We have to get you some new clothes before you start school. You know that."

"I want to wear my old clothes. What's wrong with them? Aren't they good enough for Texas?"

"Of course they are," his mom said. She inhaled slowly. Then she sunk down to sit on the stairs by the door. Jack couldn't bring himself to look at her, but she slid her finger under his chin and lifted it up until his eyes met hers.

"I know this move has been hard on you..." she started to explain.

Hard? She didn't know the half of it. Jack thought about his old apartment and the friends he'd left behind. He crossed his arms over his chest to keep from breathing funny and interrupted her before she could finish. "I'm starting middle school. At a new school. In Texas! I just want to go back to New York."

"I know you do, but we're here now, and we have to make the best of it."

"But you *wanted* to come here. You lived here before. I never wanted to come to Texas," he shouted, and he knew he had made his point when he saw his mom wince and start twirling her wedding ring. She only did that when she was really stressed out.

"I know you didn't. But you'll like it here, I promise. I did!" she said brightly. Then she pulled Jack toward the door. "Let's get going. You'll have a heat-stroke if we don't get you some new stuff to wear."

Jack let himself be pulled into the sweltering heat. It was like he had walked into a wet cotton ball, and he immediately started to sweat. New York had never been so hot, and even if it had, they could always walk down by the Hudson River and get a nice breeze. There weren't any breezes in Texas, at least not that he could tell.

They rode to the mall in silence. Jack stared out the window while his mom sang along to the radio. He didn't want to look at her, talk to her, or have anything to do with her. How could she have been so selfish, moving him to a place *she* wanted to live? She hadn't even bothered to ask what he thought.

When they finally arrived, his mom just kept talking nonstop. Jack rolled his eyes as they trekked inside. The air conditioning blasted them as they walked through the door, and Jack sighed with relief. As an added bonus, the mall music was just loud enough for him to completely zone out.

"Let's start with shoes," his mom finally said. She twirled her ring once before leading the way through the departments. They walked the men's section together and she chose an assortment of shoes for him to try while he watched in silence As they sat waiting for the sales assistant to return, his mom tried to trick him into talking by bringing up their old debate, rehashed more times than he could recall: what was the best pizza in New York City?

"You know I have to make the case for John's," she started to say.

Jack quickly blinked back tears at the thought of his favorite pizza place in New York. *This is stupid*, he thought and mashed his palm against his face. *Who cries about pizza?* He would have laughed at himself if he weren't already so sad.

Jack was startled out of his sorrow when he heard a squawking sound.

"Michelle? Is that you? Michelle Burns? I can't believe it!" a woman yelled across the shoe department as she made a beeline straight for his mom.

His mom's face tightened as the other woman approached. He looked down and saw his mom twirling her ring at a furious pace. Who was this woman? How did she know his mother?

"It IS you," the woman said as she finally reached them.

Jack's mom stood up and put her hand on Jack's shoulder, telling him it was ok for him to stay seated. The woman paused to catch her breath then continued her gushing. "I just can't believe it. I haven't seen you since high school. What are you doing here? I heard you lived in New York? Couldn't make it in the big city, huh? And this must be your son. My girls are wandering somewhere over there."

She waved her hand toward the cosmetics section. Jack peered around and saw two girls his age smearing make-up on each other as fast as they could.

Jack's mom stood there, silent. She hadn't even said "hello" even though his mom was the friendliest person he knew. That didn't stop the woman. She just kept talking as though he and his mom had acknowledged her in some way. What was going on? It seemed like they knew each other, but Jack could tell that it was clearly *not* nice to see whoever this was again. The woman didn't seem to notice though.

"Well I heard a rumor that you were back in town, but I didn't know whether or not to believe it. And now here you are, just like the rest of us. Are you living nearby? Probably renting, I would imagine. We live in the Valley View neighborhood. You probably don't know of it, it's a brand new gated community, very exclusive. But everyone still comes here to shop."

The woman paused to look over her shoulder for her daughters. She spotted them at the cosmetics counter and yelled out, "You two stop that. I can't have you getting makeup all over the training bras you need to try on."

Jack watched as the girls turned beet red and slunk away from the counter, ashamed. He looked over at his mom, who was shaking her head and looking sad.

"That should stop them, right?" The woman elbowed Jack's mom and laughed conspiratorially. She kept on talking without waiting for a response, "We should get together; I can organize a little welcome back party. I'll get in touch with you online—I can't believe we haven't linked up before now! Oh shoot, I have to run, but we'll talk again soon. Kisses!" she said in parting as she ran back toward her daughters.

"Who was that," Jack asked as he wrinkled his nose, forgetting how much his mom hated when he did that. She was still staring after the woman, who by then was loudly scolding her girls while trying to wipe-off the make-up they had applied.

"That," his mom said, as she plopped down into the seat next to him, "was the girl who bullied me all through high school." She stared off in a daze and Jack wasn't sure he had heard her correctly.

Someone had bullied his mom? His mom, who wasn't afraid of anything in New York, not even getting lost at Grand Central Station? His mom, who was always organized, knew everything Jack needed, and made the best snacks in the world? Someone had bullied his mom? All of a sudden Jack had a lump in his throat, and he didn't know what to say. He felt blindsided by the revelation that not everyone loved his mom like he did. Even when he was mad at her for making him do things like move, he still loved her.

"It was a long time ago," his mom said. "I was only a

few years older than you. I had moved schools when I was going into the eighth grade and, well, it's a hard time to move. That's part of the reason we moved now; we wanted you to be able to start middle school with everyone else, have more time before you got to high school."

Jack thought about that for a minute. "So you were trying to help me by moving here now?"

"That's right. I thought if you had the chance to start middle school with everyone else, you might not have the same experiences I did." His mom looked in the direction of the woman, who was now yelling at the lady at the cosmetics counter.

"What experiences?"

"Well, the ones that weren't so great. I was made fun of a lot, by her in particular." Jack's mom nodded in the direction of the woman. "And, despite what you think, I wasn't always as brave as I am now. Back then, the things she said really hurt my feelings."

"Didn't you have friends you could talk to?"

"Not really. Remember, I had moved to the area recently."

"Oh...but didn't other people see what was going on? Other kids, or the teachers?"

"I don't know. I don't think so. I think I hid how much it hurt. But," she paused for a moment before continuing, "I suppose going through all of that helped me become the person I am today."

"But...you're not glad that you got bullied are you?"

"No, of course not!" his mom said with a small laugh. "I guess I just look at it as, 'well, that was my experience, so I can either let that define me or I can use it to make me stronger'. I chose to use it to make me stronger, even though it wasn't a very nice experience at the time."

"I don't want to think about you being bullied," Jack said angrily. Because he didn't. It hurt him somehow, even though it had happened long before he was around. He didn't understand how people could have seen his mom being bullied and not done anything.

"You might not *want* to think about it, but you should," his mom said gently. "That way you can recognize it when you see it and make a difference."

Jack thought back over the last few months, most of which had been in New York. He thought about the dog walker who would run everyone else off the sidewalk with his pack of dogs who barked at everything. And the lady at Washington Square Park who yelled insults at anyone who wouldn't sign her petition. And the people who ran over everyone trying to get onto the subway first. They were all bullies, he realized with a start.

But his mom had always been strong and calm in those situations. She would wait on a corner for the dog walker to pass, she ignored the lady at the park while others got into shouting matches, and she never pushed her way to get onto the subway first. And usually when people saw how calm she was, they calmed down too. Jack could see what she meant about being stronger. And nicer.

Then he thought about how cruel he had been to his parents for making him move. He had been sullen and bratty every day since he had left New York. He had yelled at his mom and done everything he could to be a pain. Then a horrible realization dawned on him: his mom had twirled her ring when the woman approached her—the same way she had when he had yelled at her that very morning. His stomach sank when he thought that he might have reminded his mom of that awful woman.

And the part that made Jack feel even worse, was that other than the heat, he wasn't even minding Texas all that much. His new bedroom was enormous, they had a neighborhood pool where he could swim and make friends, and they even had a yard for their dog, so he got to play with her instead of just walking her on a leash. Truthfully, he was actually pretty happy.

"I'm sorry mom," Jack whispered as he wrapped his arms around her, not caring for once that he was at the mall and people his age might see him.

His mom hugged him back tightly. "What was that for?"

"For being a bully to you. I don't hate it here as much as I've made you think I do, and I'm sorry I've been so awful to you. I don't want to be like that lady, or the dog-walker, or the petition lady at the park, or—"

"Well that's good news," his mom said, and though she tried to hide it, Jack saw her wipe away a small tear. "Now, I think shoes can wait for another day. What do you say to investigating some Texas pizza?" she asked as she stood up.

Jack slid his hand into hers and smiled.

Questions

1. Jack is surprised to realize that his mom, who is so confident, was once a little girl who was bullied. He learns that the experiences we have when we're young often help shape who we grow up to be. What are some ways that being bullied might influence someone as they grow up?

2. Jack realizes that bullying can take many forms, and sometimes it isn't immediately obvious. Can you think of any examples from your life where you might have seen bullying taking place but not realized it until later?

3. Sometimes people act like bullies without even recognizing that they're acting that way. There are a few examples of this in this story. Can you name one? Have you ever acted like a bully without realizing it?

Eyes on the Back of My Head

CAT WOODS

MOM SAID SHE HAD EYES on the back of her head, but I didn't believe her. Not until I grew my own. Then in the hallway after science class, I saw Mike Mansky try to put a dead frog in my hoodie. I ducked and he flew over my back. The frog did too. It landed on Mike's face.

Everyone laughed, and Mike got detention for having a frog outside the science lab.

Later, I side-stepped his spit glob before it hit me in the head. Then, I weaved around Principal Stiitz just as Mike leaned forward to put a note on my back. His hand smacked a yellow sticky on Stiitz's chest.

Mike got two more days of detention for calling the principal a dork.

I didn't tell anyone about my new eyes. They were my

secret weapon against Mike Mansky. And I knew all about secrets. They lose their power when you talk about them. I certainly didn't want to lose my edge with the class bully.

I called them my super-secret laser eyes, although that might have been a mistake. As soon as I named them, I started seeing things. And not just the people behind me.

My lasers saw right into them. I couldn't see their scrambled eggs sloshing in their stomachs or their blood pumping through their veins. That would have been cool. What I saw was worse. Much worse. I saw their secrets.

I saw Layinda's heart beat for me. It got really fast whenever I walked by. I knew Toby brought his cellphone to school and that his stomach looked like a pot of rotten cabbage because of it. I even saw that Principal Stiitz hit a car in the parking lot—and he wasn't going to tell.

People were different on the inside. My super-secret laser eyes saw things my real eyes couldn't see. Like how Layinda cried every night when kids called her chubby, or that Toby brought his phone to school so the other kids would pay attention to him. He liked having friends more than he hated getting grounded.

Mr. Stiitz? I won't even talk about his insides. It's just too gross to think about.

The one that really bugged me though, was Mike Mansky. His secret made him mean. I saw things I never wanted to see. I tried to close my super-secret-laser eyes, but they didn't have lids. At night I scratched at them, but they wouldn't go away. Even the hottest shower didn't burn them out.

When Mike chucked a ball at me in gym, I let it hit me in the back of the head. Right between my eyes. It stung worse than the flu shot, but it didn't stop me from seeing.

I didn't duck out of the way when he "accidentally" spilled his lunch tray. My eyes saw right through the chicken noodle soup and chocolate pudding. I cringed at what they saw. I was lucky that Mike Mansky's lunch was the only thing that hit me.

It was just too much. That night I begged Mom for a haircut. She buzzed it right down to the nubs.

"Do you see anything unusual?" I hoped my eyes would disappear with my hair so short.

"Nothing at all." And I saw that Mom cheated on her diet with a piece of banana crème pie. Worse, she was disappointed in me. Again. This time for snapping my little sister Janie's crayons. I didn't think Mom knew about that. Or when I buried all of Janie's dolls in the backyard.

That weekend I wore a stocking hat to hide from Mom's secrets. It seemed to help. She didn't like how weird I looked, but I refused to go out of my room without it. On Monday, Principal Stiitz didn't like my new attire either. He made me put my hat in my locker—right next to the dead mouse from Mike.

I went to the bathroom to throw up. Not because of the mouse, but because of all the secrets swirling around in my head. I had to tell someone before I exploded.

That someone happened to be Mike.

He followed me into the bathroom. He wanted to laugh about the decaying mouse. Instead, I made him cry.

"I know about your secret."

Mike's face turned red, then white. His fists bunched up by his side.

"Your brother. I know what he does."

Mike growled and stepped closer to me.

"He put that mouse on your dinner plate last night."

Mike shook his head. "How could you know that?"

I almost told him about the eyes on the back of my head, but I told him the truth instead. The one my mom sees when she looks at me. "Cuz I'm a bully, too."

People are different on the inside.

Sitting on the bathroom floor, I told Mike Mansky about my super-secret laser eyes. He told me all about his big brother. We both found out I was right about secrets. They lose their power when you talk about them. And sometimes that's a good thing.

Questions

1. It would be nice to have super-secret powers to know why people do the things they do. But since we don't, how can we tell when people are mad or sad or just need a friend to listen to them?

2. The main character learns a lot of things about his classmates. What should he do about the things he knows?

3. In this story, the main character says, "People are different on the inside." What does this mean? Have you ever acted differently on the outside than the way you wanted to on the inside? Have you ever hurt someone because of that?

4. Our experiences influence the way we think about ourselves and the way we act. Why is Mike Mansky so mean? What are other reasons people might hurt others? What are some things we could do to help them stop their bad behavior?

Pork Rinds and Tacos

PRECY LARKINS

MAMA TELLS ME I HAVE to make friends. She says
this as if it's as easy as crossing the street to the
taco cart and paying the man with the funny-
looking mustache one dollar and twenty-five cents for a
greasy chicken taco. For days my sister and I have stared
out the bedroom window, watching the men with the
yellow construction helmets lined up there during lunch
and coming away with something shaped like a half moon
in their hands. They'd eat it in two seconds flat and go back
for more. The taco man would laugh and slap his jiggling
belly. My dreams would be filled with laughing mustaches
chasing after crunchy yellow moons.

Dalisay always begs me to go, but I find excuses. *It's
too hot. I'm tired. We don't have money.* But this morning,
when Dalisay found a five-dollar bill gathering dirt and

dust under the stairwell, I no longer had an excuse. She only said one word, and that was that.

Taco.

While we sneak past sleeping Mrs. Chavez, our neighbor-turned-babysitter, I try to make as much noise as possible. Dalisay shushes me, but I'm hoping we don't make it out the door. Mrs. Chavez merely grunts in her sleep, drool dribbling down her chin. The door doesn't squeak as we close it behind us.

The streets here are wide, so wide that it makes me feel jumpy. Back home, our *real* home, everything's cramped into narrow alleyways and roads bustling with jeepneys and people and litter. My palms are sweaty, but Dalisay doesn't mind as she takes my hand. The line at the taco cart snakes halfway down the block. When we finally get our turn and the taco man asks us, "Taco, si?" my mouth forgets how to work. Dalisay nods and hands the man her crumpled five-dollar bill. It's not until we're back in the apartment that I remember how to say *we want two tacos, please* in English.

Taco.

Sometimes, when I say it too fast, the c blurs until it's gone and I'm left with *ta-o*. Which is the Tagalog word for *people*. Tao, tao, tao. There are a lot of people in this city. There are a lot of people in our apartment building. And not one of them is my friend.

Mama's home from work today because it's Sunday. Dalisay has already gone out for another taco while Mama was in the shower. I can smell the leftover grease filling the air in our tiny apartment, and wonder if our mother can smell it, too. She doesn't.

"*Sige na*, you have to try. I hear there's a girl your age on the second floor. I bet she's nice." Mama winks at me as if there's some secret code between us. *Sige na.* "Come on," Mama's always saying, egging me on. But I don't see her going out of her way and befriending anybody. I don't see why I have to, and I tell her so.

"You have to make friends before school starts. It'll make it easier, promise."

"*Opo, Inay.*"

"No, no, no." Mama shakes her head. "Speak English. Only English. We're in America now. Say, 'Yes, Mom'."

"Ee-yes, mam." I know English well enough—in fact, we've learned our ABCs along with Abakada, the Filipino alphabet, since kindergarten. But while the written word is easy to understand, speaking the language is an altogether different matter.

Mama makes me repeat words and phrases from her English phrasebook until my throat feels sore and foreign to me. The strange words sting my eyes with tears of shame and fear and loneliness. When a sob catches in my chest, Mama pulls me into a hug until the ache in my heart fades a little.

"I'll make some *maruya*, okay?" Mama smiles. She knows that fried sugared bananas are my favorite. "Ligaya, will you go and check on your sister?"

"Opo...yes, mam."

"Good girl."

I share a room with my sister because there's only one other bedroom and that's where my mother sleeps. Dalisay's squatting on the floor when I come in, counting what's left of her five-dollar bill. Four quarters, two dimes, and a nickel. I'm getting better at counting money, but I don't like touching the coins. It scares me a little. Everything here scares me a little.

"There's enough for one more taco," my sister says in Tagalog, looking up. She asks me to go down with her again, just like yesterday, but this time I shake my head no.

"Fine. More for me then." Dalisay gathers up the shiny coins and holds them in her palm with reverence.

I watch her leave, her steps sure and certain, and wonder why she's not afraid.

When Papa got stabbed in the alley that twisted around our old neighborhood in Manila, Mama wouldn't talk for a week. The man who killed my father was a *hampaslupa*, a low-life looking for a small thrill and even smaller reward, the poor robbing the poor. There were no witnesses, except for the trash piling up on the sidewalks and the moon with her indifferent face. Papa was stabbed in the night for a cheap watch and a couple hundred pesos. That's about four chicken tacos in American money.

The days after that blurred into one sweltering and sticky remembrance. Relatives poured into the small chapel where my father's funeral was held. Dalisay and I were pushed from one aunt to another and ordered to bring their callused hands to our foreheads as a sign of respect. We grumbled and whined and waited for the day to be over. Little did we know that our troubles wouldn't end there.

Six months after the funeral, Mama told us we were moving. She didn't say a lot—I guess we'd kind of known it was going to happen. Her job bussing tables at a *karinderya*, a diner of sorts, didn't pay her enough to buy rice that would last us a week. We needed to start anew, so that was that. Packing only took me an hour; there wasn't much of anything to bring. Except memories.

Four layovers and a cramped leg later, we arrived at Chee-kah-goo, as Mama had called it. An aunt, who was my mother's second cousin, had taken us in, giving us an opportunity for a new beginning.

"Welcome to America!" she'd said upon our arrival, her teeth gleaming white despite the graying sun-less sky. She'd married a white, pink-faced man who owned a pizzeria located just around the corner from the apartment building we'd soon live in. I would later find out that Mama was to work at the pizzeria, bussing tables. Guess our new beginning wasn't much of a new beginning, after all.

Dalisay, who's twelve and therefore older than me, is fascinated by anything and everything in our little corner of Chicago. She lives up to her name, which means *pure*, by her simple, innocent ways. When my sister was only a year old, she fell off a window. Mama was on bed rest, her swollen belly carrying me. Dalisay tumbled down, down, onto the dirt, hitting her head on a wheelbarrow. Mama once said that if only she wasn't sick in bed that day, if only she wasn't terribly pregnant then, she could have saved Dalisay. *If only.*

In other words, it was partly my fault.

My sister functions well enough now, but there's a *dreaminess* to her that people often mistake for stupidity. I can't count the number of times I'd come home with bruised knuckles or bloodied lips. I'd always fought my sister's battles for her because she couldn't.

My name means *happiness*, though my life is anything but.

Ligaya. Happiness. I sometimes wonder if my parents made a mistake naming me.

The girl from apartment 2F has big blue eyes and frizzy white-blonde hair. Her skin's equally white and bright, so bright that sometimes it hurts my eyes when I stare at her for too long. Which I sometimes do, unable to believe my luck. Her name is Emily, and we are friends.

It happened when she and her mother came to my aunt's pizzeria. It'd been two weeks since we came to Chicago. The pizzeria was near empty, so Mama let Dalisay and me sit in one of the booths, giving us crayons and paper to draw with while she worked. Mama also set down pork rinds and a small bowl of vinegar for dipping. It was Dalisay's favorite *merienda*, or snack. She'd soak the rinds in the vinegar, the crispy skin crackling from the acidity, and shove them into her mouth two pieces at a time.

"What are you doing?" Emily had asked. Her words came out fast and blended together. All I heard was *watteryadooin*, which couldn't be found in any phrasebook known to man. But understanding clicked in place, and I told her, shyly, how I was trying to draw a unicorn.

"No," Emily said, pointing to my sister, "what is *she* doing?"

Dalisay always eats with her mouth wide open, and she was doing it then, spit and vinegar dribbling down her chin. We used to eat pork rinds on the front porch steps of our old house, and share gossip and laughter just between the two of us. Dalisay was mostly quiet, but she was a good listener. She'd turn to me, her face beaming, food smeared on her cheeks, her chin, her hands. It never bothered me before—before Emily came along, that is.

My sister wiped her hands on the hem of her shirt. "I want taco." It was the only English she'd spoken since we got here.

"Is she eating pig skin? That's so *gross!*" And, "What's wrong with her?"

The pizzeria walls closed in on me, the air reeking of garlic and sour vinegar. I pushed away the plate of pork rinds. "Hey," I said, getting up, "do you want to see the kitchen? My mom works here. I show you, okay?" Emily nodded, and that was that.

For the rest of summer, Emily and I played, inseparable. Dalisay was there, too, because Mama would sometimes drop us off at Emily's place. But my sister might as well have been invisible. With Emily, it seemed all right to laugh at Dalisay's slow and halting responses, at the way her shoelaces were always untied, at her obsession with the taco cart across the street. I figured it wasn't mean because those things we laughed about were true. Besides, Dalisay didn't seem to mind us at all.

The first day of school fills my stomach with jittery things, my breakfast of rice and fried eggs wriggling like a million maggots wanting to come out. Dalisay grips my wrist tightly, and I almost push her away but for Mama who's looking at us with worried eyes.

"Take care of your sister, okay Ligaya? You watch out for each other now." She doesn't have time to walk us to the bus stop two blocks away, but she does have time to engulf us with her mama-hen wings. She kisses the top of our heads, a prayer murmured on her lips. After our goodbyes, Mama waves once before rushing off to work.

Take care of your sister. It's always the same request. When we get to the bus stop, Emily's there, waiting for me. I pry my sister's fingers off my wrist, and bolt toward Emily without looking back.

By lunch time, Taco-Wacko spreads like a virus, infecting the entire fifth grade. Taco-Wacko is my sister. Taco-Wacko is a nightmare in a yellow cotton dress, sitting by herself at an empty table in the cafeteria, looking at me and pleading to be saved.

"L," Emily says, using the new name she's christened me with in the bus this morning. "Ignore her. You don't want to get involved, trust me."

So I sit, clenching and unclenching my fingers, watching as strangers taunt my sister with so many un-kind words. I chant *taco-taco-taco* in my head. Ta-co, Ta-o. People are mean. People are hurtful. I know Mama tells me to watch out for my sister, but Emily says I have to save my own skin. Not blood, just skin.

They surround her by the playground swings.

Papa once built Dalisay and me a swing made out of a giant black tire and thick fibrous ropes. It was still hanging from the narra tree when we left, already be-coming part of the past before we were even gone. I re-member how Dalisay stared at it, as if she could take it with her just by keeping it within her line of sight. So it doesn't come as a surprise to me that they'd attack her right when she's at her happiest, swinging on a tire swing.

Like moths to a flame, more kids join the crowd milling around my sister. Or maybe, they are the flames, and Dalisay is the moth they wish to smother and burn. I'm one of them now, standing among the tightly-packed bodies jostling for a better view. Emily's somewhere behind me, chanting *Taco-Wacko* softly under her breath. Then the crowd goes quiet. Still. As if they're waiting for someone to make the first move—the move that will determine Dalisay's fate. Will it be to her doom, or her salvation?

My hands itch, and the word *Stop* teeters on the edge of my tongue. I want to scream, *Tama na! That's enough!* But I'm afraid.

I've been afraid since Papa's mindless death. I've been afraid of Mama's hollow, tearless eyes as she shuttled us from one airport to another, her fingers clamped tight on Dalisay's wrist to prevent her from wandering off. I've been afraid of the unfamiliar words and the unfamiliar place we're supposed to call home.

I've been afraid for my sister, but mostly for myself. It was easy fighting her battles back home, when I knew what I was up against, when everything was as familiar to me as the scars on my knuckles. But here, everything's different. The faces are different.

I don't know what to do.

A rock sails in an arc above our heads, hitting Dalisay's shoulder. She winces, but she doesn't run away. I wish I could be as brave as her, but I know I'm not. Dalisay's eyes find mine in the throng, and this time, instead of pleading for help, she smiles at me.

She smiles to calm me down. She smiles to let me know I'm forgiven, even when I don't deserve her forgiveness.

More rocks fly in her direction, her fate of doom determined. *Taco-Wacko! Taco-Wacko!* Their chant is a giant pulse keeping time with my rapidly beating heart. Dalisay doesn't flinch, but she keeps her eyes on me, as if I'm the narra tree with the tire swing Papa made. As if I'm the relic of all things good in her life…eating pork rinds and vinegar under the shade of the porch awning, laughing and swapping stories, falling asleep together in the room we shared.

Blood drips down from a cut on her forehead, and yet, she's still smiling. Someone shoves her off the swing, and she falls down. And then I'm running toward my sister, my arms forming a canopy over her head to keep away the blows, even as the rocks switch aim, gunning for me.

A whistle shrills loudly, and the rock missiles stop. Footsteps scatter. I collapse on the ground next to my sister, our fingers entwining. Above us, the sky's an endless blue. I wonder if Papa's up there somewhere, watching, smiling down on us. I wonder if he knows we're okay, because we are.

Dalisay speaks first. "Ligaya? I *don't* like tacos."

"You know what? Neither do I." We turn to each other and laugh.

Questions

1. Ligaya and Dalisay came from a different country. How do you think it feels to be someplace strange and unfamiliar? Have you ever had a similar experience where you didn't know anyone and you were scared?

2. Why did Ligaya ignore Dalisay's plea for help at the cafeteria? What did Emily mean when she told Ligaya to save her own skin?

3. Ligaya said that she wasn't brave, and she didn't immediately save her sister from the kids who threw rocks at her. Why? Do you think she was brave?

Coming in 2015

Abigail Bindle
and the
SLAM BOOK
SCAM

CAT WOODS

IN WHICH I VISIT THE PRINCIPAL

I saw it as soon as I walked into homeroom. It sat on my desk, a regular blue notebook with the words "Slam Book" across the top in black letters. Something stirred in my stomach. Something with lots of wiggly legs that scrambled to get out. I wanted to vomit.

Instead, I walked down the aisle of the almost empty room. My cheeks burned. Knowing they'd draw attention like a red flag being waved at a bull, I swiped the wide-ruled notebook off my desk so I could crack the top and shove the book inside. My head followed, and I shuffled some papers around, hoping the heat would go away before the bell rang.

"Hahum." A pair of tired, brown loafers stood next to my chair. They were attached to Miss Magee.

My desktop fell with a bang. Eighteen sixth graders tittered. I was the nineteenth student, but I was the only one not laughing. Well, the only one besides Miss Magee. Her eyes blazed down at mine, and I shrunk right there on the spot. I started out that morning as the smallest girl in the whole middle school. When Miss Magee looked away, I felt even shorter.

"Abigail Bindle?" Miss Magee lumbered up the aisle, her oversized rear swaying to a beat of its own. "What do you have in your desk?"

"D…desk?" My saliva got stuck halfway down. I swallowed hard.

"Yes, Miss Bindle. Your desk."

"Just stuff, ma'am. For school." Even to my ears, I sounded like a baby first grader who got caught chewing gum. Hot tears burned my eyes. I cleared my throat and tried again. "Notebooks?"

Trisha Fox and Pamela Fey giggled.

"I saw that, Miss Bindle." For just a second, Miss Magee's eyes flickered, and she looked happy. Happy like a cat right before it pounced on a mouse. Then the flicker disappeared behind the normal beady brown color. "Bring it up here."

I, Abigail Bindle, who had never been in trouble in my entire school career, was busted. I gulped back the wiggly things in my stomach and snatched the notebook from my desk. All the way to the front of the classroom, I cursed the stupid blue book. I cursed whoever had come up with slam books. I cursed my classmates for making a big deal of them. Most of all, I cursed myself for wanting, just once, to peek inside and see what everyone thought about everyone else. Especially me.

But now, when I finally got my turn with the sixth grade slam book, Miss Magee had to be there. And now, I was busted.

I stood in front of Miss Magee. She leaned heavily against her desk; her right cheek half on-half off the wooden top. I held the notebook toward her, but she didn't take it. "Open it to the first page."

The stomach wigglies threatened to crawl up my throat and come spewing out my mouth.

"Now read it to the class."

"Finally." Even with my back turned, I recognized Pamela's voice. She led the cheer team, so everyone in all of Pebble Creek Middle School recognized her voice and the way the words slipped out of her mouth like they were coated with soap. At that moment, I hated the way that one word bubbled up, getting louder just before it popped into the quiet classroom.

Behind me, kids laughed.

"It's about time," someone whispered back. Zack Pendleton. Pamela's lapdog. I could almost hear him wagging his tail, hoping for a head pat from her.

"Goody two shoes." That was Trisha, Pamela's best friend.

My humiliation was complete. I didn't need the slam book to find out what anyone thought of Abigail Bindle, honor student and geek extraordinaire. I opened the book. The handwriting looped and scrawled across the page. My heart stuttered, and the wigglies turned to sponges. They soaked up my saliva and my words. I shook my head.

"Oh, for heaven's sake." Miss Magee snatched the notebook from my hands. Her eyes scanned the page. The beady brown orbs frantically searched back and forth and back and forth again, as if the words would suddenly morph and say Pamela Fey was a horrible snob or Adam Aimsly ran like a duck.

But they couldn't, because in that second before Miss Magee snatched the book away from me, I saw her name. Magdalene Magee. I also saw the slam. My stomach churned with liquid mush. My legs wobbled, and I waited for Miss Magee's blast of anger.

I didn't have long to wait. Her words curled around me, so cold the wiggly mush froze into a hard ball in the pit of my stomach.

"You know these are against school rules, don't you?"

I nodded. For the first time in history, all nineteen

students in room 107 kept their mouths shut. Even Pamela Fey.

"You're looking at detention for the rest of the year." Miss Magee glared at me with rabid eyes and smacked the book against my shoulder. "Detention and suspension."

She turned her anger on the class. Spittle flew, spraying the front row. "It will be detention, suspension, and sixth grade all over again for anyone who signed this book. For anyone who even looked at it."

Miss Magee pointed her sausagey finger at me and then the hall.

By the time I reached Principal Osmond's office, I was more of a mess than his room. Cluttered bookshelves lined the walls. A thick layer of dust coated everything except an arc on his desk where his arms swept it clean. Papers poked out of half-closed file cabinets. My folder sat in the middle of his desk, just under his folded hands.

He nodded to an orange chair in the corner. The stuffing seeped out of a crack in the vinyl and felt lumpy when I sat down. Still shaking from humiliation, I pushed my elbows onto the metal armrests and clamped my lips shut to keep my chattering teeth from chewing up my tongue.

After an impossibly long minute, Miss Magee stormed into the office without knocking. I thought of the first line in the slam book and silently agreed. She did look like an alien octopus, right down to her pulsating jowls. Ignoring Principal Osmond's nod at the matching vinyl chair next to me, she slammed the notebook onto his desk.

"There it is," she said with that pouncing cat look. "Just like I told you."

Again, Principal Osmond nodded toward the chair. Miss Magee wedged herself between the armrests and leaned forward to tap the notebook. When she did, the whole chair inched forward with each rap of her knuckles.

Principal Osmond opened the battered blue book. From where I sat, I could see Miss Magee's name written in block letters. Below that, writing filled half the page. I loved all kinds of brain teasers and could read upside down and backwards without a problem. It helped that the handwriting was open and neat. I quickly scanned past the pulsating octopus to the name of the slammer.

My name.

Abigail Bindle. I sucked in a deep breath.

Principal Osmond's eyes ping-ponged across the page as he read the entire insult. Miss Magee tried to interrupt him, but he held up his hand to silence her. Her face turned purpley red and her cheeks quivered. Like me, she seemed to be holding her breath.

Principal Osmond flipped through the notebook. Each page had the same heading. Magdalene Magee. Each page held a scribbled paragraph.

My breath rushed out along with my disappointment. *How come nobody wrote about creepy Zack Pendleton or how Trisha's bad breath could curdle milk into cottage cheese? And where was my name?*

I did not spend an entire year worrying about the slam book, only to find out somebody thought Miss Magee looked like an alien. I didn't care about Miss Magee. I wanted to know about Adam and Trisha and Pamela. I wanted to read the dirt, the romance, the secrets. And most of all, I wanted to read about me.

This thought niggled in my brain as the pages fanned by. Principal Osmond must have had the same niggle. "What kind of slam book is this?"

Having never seen a slam book in my life, I shrugged. "I don't know. I've never seen it before."

Miss Magee's eyes bored into me. "Your name is in there."

"My point exactly." Principal Osmond slid the book toward me.

I riffled through the pages, looking for signatures, but found none. I did find a little octopus in the bottom corner. As the pages fell, the octopus came alive like an old-fashioned cartoon. "Mine's the only name in here."

"But it's there." Miss Magee spluttered and her face turned blue. She looked just like the dancing octopus.

Principal Osmond held up his hand. "Miss Magee, have you ever seen a slam book where only one person is slammed?"

She shifted in her chair. The chair shifted with her. She mumbled something just as the vinyl escaped from under her. Miss Magee's face turned three shades bluer.

"I'm sorry. I didn't quite hear that." Principal Osmond's cheeks turned red. He kept his eyes down at the book to avoid looking at Miss Magee.

She kept her eyes on his hands. "I said I've never seen a slam book before."

Principal Osmond pushed a piece of paper and pen my way. "Sign your name, please."

I did. The signatures matched—mostly—although a few funny points stuck out where there should have been round-ed tops. Also, the words looked like they had been squished.

"It looks like someone tried to copy it."

"I expected you to say as much. You kids always deny your culpability." Principal Osmond opened my file and scratched something on a piece of paper inside. His hand covered my view, and I couldn't read the note.

I gulped down the bile. Somebody had faked my name. Somebody placed that slam book on my desk so I would take the fall. And now, I had my first note in my cumulative file. "That's not fair. Someone set me up."

Principal Osmond nodded. "I suppose you could have been framed."

"By who?"

"By whom?" He shot me a teacher look and shrugged. "When you figure it out, let me know. Until then, you have one week of community service for disrespecting a teacher and having a slam book in your possession. Well, a week of school service, anyway."

I shuddered at the thought of emptying the garbage cans after lunch or scrubbing the graffiti off the bathroom stalls. I needed to clear my name before anyone saw me acting like an ordinary delinquent. I reached for the slam book. "I'll need this to get a better look at the entry."

Miss Magee whipped toward me, her whole chair screeching across the tile floor. "I should have it. After all, it's my slam book."

I turned to Principal Osmond. "I'll need to see the writing to…"

"…read about me." Miss Magee's voice moved down the scale an octave. "Laugh about me. Share it with your friends."

I snorted. "If I had friends, I wouldn't be sitting here right now, framed for something I didn't do."

"She has a point," Principal Osmond said to Miss Magee. "It's hard to share with friends when you don't have any."

I cleared my throat to remind them I was still in the room. "I have one."

They stopped talking and stared at me. Principal Osmond shrugged. "I suppose one page can't hurt. Especially since you wrote it."

While I'd already memorized the words of a few other slams, I wanted more than one page to compare handwriting, but I wasn't going to fight. Not with Miss Magee shooting darts at me with her eyes.

In the end, Principal Osmond photocopied the page for me, slid the slam book into my file, and shoved the bulging folder in the cabinet. I left his office with the photo copy, a head full of other slams, and a yellow slip letting my mom know I had school service for the first week of summer.

Unless, of course, I solved the mystery of the slam book before school let out in five days.

About the Authors

Linda Brewer

Linda Brewer teaches second grade and is halfway toward her black belt in Tae Kwon Do. She lives with her two sons in a suburb of Cleveland, and writes books in her spare time. More of her writing can be found at <u>layinda.wordpress.com</u>.

Steven Carman

Steven Carman is a writer of middle grade and young adult fiction, with a focus on sports stories that deal with difficult issues many children face, such as abuse and bullying. A former counselor at a group home for mentally ill adults, Steven now works as a marketing manager for one of the world's largest membership organizations. He has been a baseball enthusiast since his T-ball playing days, and while his dream of playing in the Major Leagues is long gone, he's now chasing a dream to entertain sports fans through his writing. His first novel, *Battery Brothers*, was published in March 2014 by Elephant's Bookshelf Press. Steven lives in New York with his wife, two kids, and two cats.

Eden Grey

Eden Jean Grey has always been a little different. Eden is a teen librarian, an anime fan, a YA Lit reviewer, Michigan-native, and proud pet of a 3-year-old dachshund. She lives in Northern Kentucky, where she reads, writes, sews, and blogs. You can find her on Twitter (@edynjean). Her blog address is edynjean.wordpress.com.

K.R. Smith

K.R. Smith is an Information Technology specialist and writer living in the Washington, D.C., area. While mainly interested in writing short stories, he occasionally delves into poetry, songwriting, and the visual arts. Samples of his other works and additional links to more are available at www.theworldofkrsmith.com.

Precy Larkins

Precy Larkins grew up in the Philippines eating pork rinds with her friends. She now lives in Utah with her husband and three children (they like pork rinds, too). She's a Young Adult writer represented by Julia A. Weber of J.A. Weber Literaturagentur GmbH, and has had adult short stories published on Hogglepot.com and in the *Winter's Regret* anthology by Elephant's Bookshelf Press. She blogs at precylarkins.wordpress.com and tweets as @precylarkins.

If she could be a superhero, she'd like powers that could stop meanies from making fun of people. No capes, though. You can also find her on Goodreads and Tumblr (precylarkins. tumblr.com).

Sarah Tregay

Raised without television, Sarah Tregay started writing her own middle grade novels after she had read all of the ones in the library. She later discovered YA books, but never did make it to the adult section. Sarah is the author of two young adult novels. Both *Love and Leftovers* and *Fan Art* are published by Katherine Tegen Books/HarperCollins. Sarah lives in Eagle, Idaho, with her husband, two Boston Terriers, and an appaloosa named Mr. Pots. You can find her online at www.sarahtregay.com, www. facebook.com/sarahtregaybooks, and www.pinterest.com/ sarahtregay.

Cat Woods

Cat Woods has a passion for pirates, chai tea, and underdogs. She gathers novel fodder from captaining her crew of four children, two dogs, and one Dear Hubby. Her middle grade novel, *Abigail Bindle and the Slam Book Scam*, is slated for release in 2015 from Elephant's Bookshelf Press. When she's not writing, Cat hangs out in her garden watching her favorite birds and dreaming of the ocean from her home in land-locked Minnesota. She keeps track of her writing projects at www.catwoodsbooks.com and blogs about bugs, bullies, and other cool stuff at Cat 4 Kids: www.catwoodskids.com.

Lauren Neil

Lauren Neil decided that she wanted to become a lawyer at eight years old because she was good at reading, writing, and arguing. She became a lawyer, but decided that reading and writing are a lot more fun when kids are involved, and arguing is generally no fun at all. She was inspired to write this story by thinking about how she would one day explain her experiences with bullying to her son. When she isn't writing she can be found spending time with her husband Pat, her son Jack, and their spoiled English Cocker Spaniel, Shelby, in Austin, Texas. You can follow Lauren on Twitter @BStBibliophile.